Yolanda Suarez-Balcazar, PhD
Gary W. Harper, PhD, MPH
Editors

D1615895

Empowerment and Participatory Evaluation of Community Interventions: Multiple Benefits

Empowerment and Participatory Evaluation of Community Interventions: Multiple Benefits has been co-published simultaneously as *Journal of Prevention & Intervention in the Community*, Volume 26, Number 2 2003.

*Pre-publication
REVIEWS,
COMMENTARIES,
EVALUATIONS . . .*

"**U**SEFUL. . . . Draws together diverse chapters that uncover the how and why of empowerment and participatory evaluation while offering exemplary case studies showing the challenges and successes of this community value-based evaluation model."

Anne E. Brodsky, PhD
*Associate Professor of Psychology
University of Maryland
Baltimore County*

The Haworth Press, Inc.

Empowerment and Participatory Evaluation of Community Interventions: Multiple Benefits

Empowerment and Participatory Evaluation of Community Interventions: Multiple Benefits has been co-published simultaneously as *Journal of Prevention & Intervention in the Community*, Volume 26, Number 2 2003.

The *Journal of Prevention & Intervention in the Community*™ Monographic "Separates" (formerly the *Prevention in Human Services* series)*

For information on previous issues of *Prevention in Human Services*, edited by Robert E. Hess, please contact: The Haworth Press, Inc., 10 Alice Street, Binghamton, NY 13904-1580 USA.

Below is a list of "separates," which in serials librarianship means a special issue simultaneously published as a special journal issue or double-issue *and* as a "separate" hardbound monograph. (This is a format which we also call a "DocuSerial.")

"Separates" are published because specialized libraries or professionals may wish to purchase a specific thematic issue by itself in a format which can be separately cataloged and shelved, as opposed to purchasing the journal on an on-going basis. Faculty members may also more easily consider a "separate" for classroom adoption.

"Separates" are carefully classified separately with the major book jobbers so that the journal tie-in can be noted on new book order slips to avoid duplicate purchasing.

You may wish to visit Haworth's website at . . .

http://www.HaworthPress.com

. . . to search our online catalog for complete tables of contents of these separates and related publications.

You may also call 1-800-HAWORTH (outside US/Canada: 607-722-5857), or Fax 1-800-895-0582 (outside US/Canada: 607-771-0012), or e-mail at:

docdelivery@haworthpress.com

Empowerment and Participatory Evaluation of Community Interventions: Multiple Benefits, edited by Yolanda Suarez-Balcazar, PhD, and Gary W. Harper, PhD, MPH (Vol. 26, No. 2, 2003). *"USEFUL. . . . Draws together diverse chapters that uncover the how and why of empowerment and participatory evaluation while offering exemplary case studies showing the challenges and successes of this community value-based evaluation model." (Anne E. Brodsky, PhD, Associate Professor of Psychology, University of Maryland Baltimore County)*

Traumatic Stress and Its Aftermath: Cultural, Community, and Professional Contexts, edited by Sandra S. Lee, PhD (Vol. 26, No. 1, 2003). *Explores risk and protective factors for traumatic stress, emphasizing the impact of cumulative/multiple trauma in a variety of populations, including therapists themselves.*

Culture, Peers, and Delinquency, edited by Clifford O'Donnell, PhD (Vol. 25, No. 2, 2003). *"TIMELY . . . . OF VALUE TO BOTH STUDENTS AND PROFESSIONALS. . . . Demonstrates how peers can serve as a pathway to delinquency from a multiethnic perspective. The discussion of ethnic, racial, and gender differences challenges the field to reconsider assessment, treatment, and preventative approaches." (Donald Meichenbaum, PhD, Distinguished Professor Emeritus, University of Waterloo, Ontario, Canada; Research Director, The Melissa Institute for Violence Prevention and the Treatment of Victims of Violence, Miami, Florida)*

Prevention and Intervention Practice in Post-Apartheid South Africa, edited by Vijé Franchi, PhD, and Norman Duncan, PhD, consulting editor (Vol. 25, No.1, 2003). *"Highlights the way in which preventive and curative interventions serve–or do not serve–the ideals of equality, empowerment, and participation. . . . Revolutionizes our way of thinking about and teaching socio-pedagogical action in the context of exclusion." (Dr. Altay A. Manço, Scientific Director, Institute of Research, Training, and Action on Migrations, Belgium)*

Community Interventions to Create Change in Children, edited by Lorna H. London, PhD (Vol. 24, No. 2, 2002). *"ILLUSTRATES CREATIVE APPROACHES to prevention and intervention with at-risk youth. . . . Describes multiple methods to consider in the design, implementation, and evaluation of programs." (Susan D. McMahon, PhD, Assistant Professor, Department of Psychology, DePaul University)*

Preventing Youth Access to Tobacco, edited by Leonard A. Jason, PhD, and Steven B. Pokorny, PhD (Vol. 24, No. 1, 2002). *"Explores cutting-edge issues in youth access research methodology. . . . Provides a thorough review of the tobacco control literature and detailed analysis of the methodological issues presented by community interventions to increase the effectiveness of to-*

bacco control. . . . Challenges widespread assumptions about the dynamics of youth access programs and the requirements for long-term success." (*John A. Gardiner, PhD, LLB, Consultant to the 2000 Surgeon General's Report* Reducing Youth Access to Tobacco *and to the National Cancer Institute's evaluation of the ASSIST program*)

The Transition from Welfare to Work: Processes, Challenges, and Outcomes, edited by Sharon Telleen, PhD, and Judith V. Sayad (Vol. 23, No. 1/2, 2002). *A comprehensive examination of the welfare-to-work initiatives surrounding the major reform of United States welfare legislation in 1996.*

Prevention Issues for Women's Health in the New Millennium, edited by Wendee M. Wechsberg, PhD (Vol. 22, No. 2, 2001). *"Helpful to service providers as well as researchers . . . A USEFUL ANCILLARY TEXTBOOK for courses addressing women's health issues. Covers a wide range of health issues affecting women."* (*Sherry Deren, PhD, Director, Center for Drug Use and HIV Research, National Drug Research Institute, New York City*)

Workplace Safety: Individual Differences in Behavior, edited by Alice F. Stuhlmacher, PhD, and Douglas F. Cellar, PhD (Vol. 22, No. 1, 2001). Workplace Safety: Individual Differences in Behavior *examines safety behavior and outlines practical interventions to help increase safety awareness. Individual differences are relevant to a variety of settings, including the workplace, public spaces, and motor vehicles. This book takes a look at ways of defining and measuring safety as well as a variety of individual differences like gender, job knowledge, conscientiousness, self-efficacy, risk avoidance, and stress tolerance that are important in creating safety interventions and improving the selection and training of employees.* Workplace Safety *takes an incisive look at these issues with a unique focus on the way individual differences in people impact safety behavior in the real world.*

People with Disabilities: Empowerment and Community Action, edited by Christopher B. Keys, PhD, and Peter W. Dowrick, PhD (Vol. 21, No. 2, 2001). *"Timely and useful . . . provides valuable lessons and guidance for everyone involved in the disability movement. This book is a must-read for researchers and practitioners interested in disability rights issues!"* (*Karen M. Ward, EdD, Director, Center for Human Development; Associate Professor, University of Alaska, Anchorage*)

Family Systems/Family Therapy: Applications for Clinical Practice, edited by Joan D. Atwood, PhD (Vol. 21, No. 1, 2001). *Examines family therapy issues in the context of the larger systems of health, law, and education and suggests ways family therapists can effectively use an intersystems approach.*

HIV/AIDS Prevention: Current Issues in Community Practice, edited by Doreen D. Salina, PhD (Vol. 19, No. 1, 2000). *Helps researchers and psychologists explore specific methods of improving HIV/AIDS prevention research.*

Educating Students to Make-a-Difference: Community-Based Service Learning, edited by Joseph R. Ferrari, PhD, and Judith G. Chapman, PhD (Vol. 18, No. 1/2, 1999). *"There is something here for everyone interested in the social psychology of service-learning."* (*Frank Bernt, PhD, Associate Professor, St. Joseph's University*)

Program Implementation in Preventive Trials, edited by Joseph A. Durlak and Joseph R. Ferrari, PhD (Vol. 17, No. 2, 1998). *"Fills an important gap in preventive research. . . . Highlights an array of important questions related to implementation and demonstrates just how good community-based intervention programs can be when issues related to implementation are taken seriously."* (*Judy Primavera, PhD, Associate Professor of Psychology, Fairfield University, Fairfield, Connecticut*)

Preventing Drunk Driving, edited by Elsie R. Shore, PhD, and Joseph R. Ferrari, PhD (Vol. 17, No. 1, 1998). *"A must read for anyone interested in reducing the needless injuries and death caused by the drunk driver."* (*Terrance D. Schiavone, President, National Commission Against Drunk Driving, Washington, DC*)

Manhood Development in Urban African-American Communities, edited by Roderick J. Watts, PhD, and Robert J. Jagers (Vol. 16, No. 1/2, 1998). *"Watts and Jagers provide the much-needed foundational and baseline information and research that begins to philosophically and empirically validate the importance of understanding culture, oppression, and gender when working* *with males in urban African-American communities." (Paul Hill, Jr., MSW, LISW, ACSW, East End Neighborhood House, Cleveland, Ohio)*

Diversity Within the Homeless Population: Implications for Intervention, edited by Elizabeth M. Smith, PhD, and Joseph R. Ferrari, PhD (Vol. 15, No. 2, 1997). *"Examines why homelessness is increasing, as well as treatment options, case management techniques, and community intervention programs that can be used to prevent homelessness." (American Public Welfare Association)*

Education in Community Psychology: Models for Graduate and Undergraduate Programs, edited by Clifford R. O'Donnell, PhD, and Joseph R. Ferrari, PhD (Vol. 15, No. 1, 1997). *"An invaluable resource for students seeking graduate training in community psychology . . . [and will] also serve faculty who want to improve undergraduate teaching and graduate programs." (Marybeth Shinn, PhD, Professor of Psychology and Coordinator, Community Doctoral Program, New York University, New York, New York)*

Adolescent Health Care: Program Designs and Services, edited by John S. Wodarski, PhD, Marvin D. Feit, PhD, and Joseph R. Ferrari, PhD (Vol. 14, No. 1/2, 1997). *Devoted to helping practitioners address the problems of our adolescents through the use of preventive interventions based on sound empirical data.*

Preventing Illness Among People with Coronary Heart Disease, edited by John D. Piette, PhD, Robert M. Kaplan, PhD, and Joseph R. Ferrari, PhD (Vol. 13, No. 1/2, 1996). *"A useful contribution to the interaction of physical health, mental health, and the behavioral interventions for patients with CHD." (Public Health: The Journal of the Society of Public Health)*

Sexual Assault and Abuse: Sociocultural Context of Prevention, edited by Carolyn F. Swift, PhD* (Vol. 12, No. 2, 1995). *"Delivers a cornucopia for all who are concerned with the primary prevention of these damaging and degrading acts." (George J. McCall, PhD, Professor of Sociology and Public Administration, University of Missouri)*

International Approaches to Prevention in Mental Health and Human Services, edited by Robert E. Hess, PhD, and Wolfgang Stark* (Vol. 12, No. 1, 1995). *Increases knowledge of prevention strategies from around the world.*

Self-Help and Mutual Aid Groups: International and Multicultural Perspectives, edited by Francine Lavoie, PhD, Thomasina Borkman, PhD, and Benjamin Gidron* (Vol. 11, No. 1/2, 1995). *"A helpful orientation and overview, as well as useful data and methodological suggestions." (International Journal of Group Psychotherapy)*

Prevention and School Transitions, edited by Leonard A. Jason, PhD, Karen E. Danner, and Karen S. Kurasaki, MA* (Vol. 10, No. 2, 1994). *"A collection of studies by leading ecological and systems-oriented theorists in the area of school transitions, describing the stressors, personal resources available, and coping strategies among different groups of children and adolescents undergoing school transitions." (Reference & Research Book News)*

Religion and Prevention in Mental Health: Research, Vision, and Action, edited by Kenneth I. Pargament, PhD, Kenneth I. Maton, PhD, and Robert E. Hess, PhD* (Vol. 9, No. 2 & Vol. 10, No. 1, 1992). *"The authors provide an admirable framework for considering the important, yet often overlooked, differences in theological perspectives." (Family Relations)*

Families as Nurturing Systems: Support Across the Life Span, edited by Donald G. Unger, PhD, and Douglas R. Powell, PhD* (Vol. 9, No. 1, 1991). *"A useful book for anyone thinking about alternative ways of delivering a mental health service." (British Journal of Psychiatry)*

Ethical Implications of Primary Prevention, edited by Gloria B. Levin, PhD, and Edison J. Trickett, PhD* (Vol. 8, No. 2, 1991). *"A thoughtful and thought-provoking summary of ethical issues related to intervention programs and community research." (Betty Tableman, MPA, Director, Division. of Prevention Services and Demonstration Projects, Michigan Department of Mental Health, Lansing) Here is the first systematic and focused treatment of the ethical implications of primary prevention practice and research.*

Career Stress in Changing Times, edited by James Campbell Quick, PhD, MBA, Robert E. Hess, PhD, Jared Hermalin, PhD, and Jonathan D. Quick, MD* (Vol. 8, No. 1, 1990). *"A well-orga-*

nized book. . . . It deals with planning a career and career changes and the stresses involved." *(American Association of Psychiatric Administrators)*

Prevention in Community Mental Health Centers, edited by Robert E. Hess, PhD, and John Morgan, PhD* (Vol. 7, No. 2, 1990). *"A fascinating bird's-eye view of six significant programs of preventive care which have survived the rise and fall of preventive psychiatry in the U.S." (British Journal of Psychiatry)*

Protecting the Children: Strategies for Optimizing Emotional and Behavioral Development, edited by Raymond P. Lorion, PhD* (Vol. 7, No. 1, 1990). *"This is a masterfully conceptualized and edited volume presenting theory-driven, empirically based, developmentally oriented prevention." (Michael C. Roberts, PhD, Professor of Psychology, The University of Alabama)*

The National Mental Health Association: Eighty Years of Involvement in the Field of Prevention, edited by Robert E. Hess, PhD, and Jean DeLeon, PhD* (Vol. 6, No. 2, 1989). *"As a family life educator interested in both the history of the field, current efforts, and especially the evaluation of programs, I find this book quite interesting. I enjoyed reviewing it and believe that I will return to it many times. It is also a book I will recommend to students." (Family Relations)*

A Guide to Conducting Prevention Research in the Community: First Steps, by James G. Kelly, PhD, Nancy Dassoff, PhD, Ira Levin, PhD, Janice Schreckengost, MA, AB, Stephen P. Stelzner, PhD, and B. Eileen Altman, PhD* (Vol. 6, No. 1, 1989). *"An invaluable compendium for the prevention practitioner, as well as the researcher, laying out the essentials for developing effective prevention programs in the community. . . . This is a book which should be in the prevention practitioner's library, to read, re-read, and ponder." (The Community Psychologist)*

Prevention: Toward a Multidisciplinary Approach, edited by Leonard A. Jason, PhD, Robert D. Felner, PhD, John N. Moritsugu, PhD, and Robert E. Hess, PhD* (Vol. 5, No. 2, 1987). *"Will not only be of intellectual value to the professional but also to students in courses aimed at presenting a refreshingly comprehensive picture of the conceptual and practical relationships between community and prevention." (Seymour B. Sarason, Associate Professor of Psychology, Yale University)*

Prevention and Health: Directions for Policy and Practice, edited by Alfred H. Katz, PhD, Jared A. Hermalin, PhD, and Robert E. Hess, PhD* (Vol. 5, No. 1, 1987). *Read about the most current efforts being undertaken to promote better health.*

The Ecology of Prevention: Illustrating Mental Health Consultation, edited by James G. Kelly, PhD, and Robert E. Hess, PhD* (Vol. 4, No. 3/4, 1987). *"Will provide the consultant with a very useful framework and the student with an appreciation for the time and commitment necessary to bring about lasting changes of a preventive nature." (The Community Psychologist)*

Beyond the Individual: Environmental Approaches and Prevention, edited by Abraham Wandersman, PhD, and Robert E. Hess, PhD* (Vol. 4, No. 1/2, 1985). *"This excellent book has immediate appeal for those involved with environmental psychology . . . likely to be of great interest to those working in the areas of community psychology, planning, and design." (Australian Journal of Psychology)*

Prevention: The Michigan Experience, edited by Betty Tableman, MPA, and Robert E. Hess, PhD* (Vol. 3, No. 4, 1985). *An in-depth look at one state's outstanding prevention programs.*

Studies in Empowerment: Steps Toward Understanding and Action, edited by Julian Rappaport, Carolyn Swift, and Robert E. Hess, PhD* (Vol. 3, No. 2/3, 1984). *"Provides diverse applications of the empowerment model to the promotion of mental health and the prevention of mental illness." (Prevention Forum Newsline)*

Aging and Prevention: New Approaches for Preventing Health and Mental Health Problems in Older Adults, edited by Sharon P. Simson, Laura Wilson, Jared Hermalin, PhD, and Robert E. Hess, PhD* (Vol. 3, No. 1, 1983). *"Highly recommended for professionals and laymen interested in modern viewpoints and techniques for avoiding many physical and mental health problems of the elderly. Written by highly qualified contributors with extensive experience in their respective fields." (The Clinical Gerontologist)*

Monographs "Separates" list continued at the back

Empowerment and Participatory Evaluation of Community Interventions: Multiple Benefits

Yolanda Suarez-Balcazar, PhD
Gary W. Harper, PhD, MPH
Editors

Empowerment and Participatory Evaluation of Community Interventions: Multiple Benefits has been co-published simultaneously as *Journal of Prevention & Intervention in the Community*, Volume 26, Number 2 2003.

The Haworth Press, Inc.

New York • London • Victoria (AU)
www.HaworthPress.com

Empowerment and Participatory Evaluation of Community Interventions: Multiple Benefits has been co-published simultaneously as *Journal of Prevention & Intervention in the Community*™, Volume 26, Number 2 2003.

The Haworth Press, Inc., 10 Alice Street, Binghamton, NY 13904-1580 USA

Cover design by Jennifer M. Gaska

Library of Congress Cataloging-in-Publication Data

Empowerment and participatory evaluation of community interventions: multiple benefits / Yolanda Suarez-Balcazar, Gary W. Harper, co-editors.
    p. cm.
    "Has been co-published simultaneously as Journal of prevention & intervention in the community, volume 26, number 2, 2003."
    Includes bibliographical references and index.
    ISBN 0-7890-2208-7 (alk. paper) – ISBN 0-7890-2209-5 (softcover: alk. paper)
    1. Social service–Evaluation–Citizen participation. 2. Human services–Evaluation–Citizen participation. 3. Community health services–Evaluation–Citizen participation. 4. Evaluation research (Social action programs)–Citizen participation. I. Suarez-Balcazar, Yolanda. II. Harper, Gary W. III. Journal of prevention & intervention in the community.
HV40.E47 2003
361.2'068–dc21

                                                      2003011595

Indexing, Abstracting & Website/Internet Coverage

This section provides you with a list of major indexing & abstracting services. That is to say, each service began covering this periodical during the year noted in the right column. Most Websites which are listed below have indicated that they will either post, disseminate, compile, archive, cite or alert their own Website users with research-based content from this work. (This list is as current as the copyright date of this publication.)

Abstracting, Website/Indexing Coverage . . . . Year When Coverage Began

- *Behavioral Medicine Abstracts* 1996

- *CINAHL (Cumulative Index to Nursing & Allied Health Literature), in print, EBSCO, and Silverplatter, Data-Star, and PaperChase. (Support materials include Subject Heading List, Database Search Guide, and instructional video). <http://www.cinahl.com>* 2003

- *CNPIEC Reference Guide: Chinese National Directory of Foreign Periodicals* 1996

- *Educational Research Abstracts (ERA) (online database) <http://www.tandf.co.uk/era>* 2002

- *EMBASE/Excerpta Medica Secondary Publishing Division <http://www.elsevier.nl>* 1996

- *e-psyche, LLC <http://www.e-psyche.net>* 2001

- *Family & Society Studies Worldwide <http://www.nisc.com>* 1996

- *Family Index Database <http://www.familyscholar.com>* 2003

- *FINDEX <http://www.publist.com>* 1999

(continued)

- *Gay & Lesbian Abstracts <http://www.nisc.com>* **2000**

- *HealthPromis* **1997**

- *IBZ International Bibliography of Periodical Literature*
    <http://www.saur.de> **1996**

- *MANTIS (Manual, Alternative, and Natural Therapy)*
    MANTIS is available through three database vendors:
    Ovid, Dialog, & DataStar <http://www.healthindex.com> **2000**

- *National Center for Chronic Disease Prevention*
    & Health Promotion (NCCDPHP) **1999**

- *National Clearinghouse on Child Abuse & Neglect*
    Information Documents Database
    <http://www.calib.com/nccanch> **1996**

- *NIAAA Alcohol and Alcohol Problems Science Database (ETOH)*
    <http://etoh.niaaa.nih.gov> **1996**

- *Psychological Abstracts (PsycINFO)*
    <http://www.apa.org> **1998**

- *Referativnyi Zhurnal (Abstracts Journal of the All-Russian*
    Institute of Scientific and Technical Information-in Russian). . . . **1996**

- *Social Services Abstracts <http://www.csa.com>* **1996**

- *Social Work Abstracts*
    <http://www.silverplatter.com/catalog/swab.htm>. **1996**

- *SocIndex (EBSCO)* **2003**

- *Sociological Abstracts (SA) <http://www.csa.com>* **1996**

- *SwetsNet <http://www.swetsnet.com>* **2001**

- *Violence and Abuse Abstracts: A Review of Current*
    Literature on Interpersonal Violence (VAA) **1996**

(continued)

*Special Bibliographic Notes related to special journal issues
(separates) and indexing/abstracting:*

- indexing/abstracting services in this list will also cover material in any "separate" that is co-published simultaneously with Haworth's special thematic journal issue or DocuSerial. Indexing/abstracting usually covers material at the article/chapter level.
- monographic co-editions are intended for either non-subscribers or libraries which intend to purchase a second copy for their circulating collections.
- monographic co-editions are reported to all jobbers/wholesalers/approval plans. The source journal is listed as the "series" to assist the prevention of duplicate purchasing in the same manner utilized for books-in-series.
- to facilitate user/access services all indexing/abstracting services are encouraged to utilize the co-indexing entry note indicated at the bottom of the first page of each article/chapter/contribution.
- this is intended to assist a library user of any reference tool (whether print, electronic, online, or CD-ROM) to locate the monographic version if the library has purchased this version but not a subscription to the source journal.
- individual articles/chapters in any Haworth publication are also available through the Haworth Document Delivery Service (HDDS).

Empowerment and Participatory Evaluation of Community Interventions: Multiple Benefits

CONTENTS

Community-Based Approaches to Empowerment
 and Participatory Evaluation   1
  Yolanda Suarez-Balcazar
  Gary W. Harper

Implementing an Outcomes Model in the Participatory
 Evaluation of Community Initiatives   5
  Yolanda Suarez-Balcazar
  Lucía Orellana-Damacela
  Nelson Portillo
  Aparna Sharma
  Mindy Lanum

Building Capacity for Participatory Evaluation
 Within Community Initiatives   21
  Stephen B. Fawcett
  Renée Boothroyd
  Jerry A. Schultz
  Vincent T. Francisco
  Valorie Carson
  Roderick Bremby

Promoting Program Success and Fulfilling Accountability
    Requirements in a Statewide Community-Based Initiative:
    Challenges, Progress, and Lessons Learned   37
        Paul Flaspohler
        Abraham Wandersman
        Dana Keener
        Kathryn North Maxwell
        April Ace
        Arlene Andrews
        Baron Holmes

Collaborative Process Evaluation: Enhancing Community
    Relevance and Cultural Appropriateness in HIV Prevention   53
        Gary W. Harper
        Richard Contreras
        Audrey Bangi
        Ana Pedraza

Collaborative Program Development and Evaluation:
    A Case Study in Conflict Resolution Education   71
        Carolyn G. Benne
        Wendy M. Garrard

Empowerment Evaluation of a Youth Leadership
    Training Program   89
        Aparna Sharma
        Yolanda Suarez-Balcazar
        Matthew Baetke

Index   105

ABOUT THE EDITORS

Yolanda Suarez-Balcazar, PhD, is Associate Professor in the Department of Occupational Therapy at the University of Illinois at Chicago. She was trained as a community psychologist at the University of Kansas. Her research interest and expertise include the study of participatory and empowerment evaluation methods, university-community partnerships, needs assessment methodologies and issues of multicultural training and diversity. She has a number of publications and professional presentations in these areas. She has worked with over 30 community-based organizations in the implementation of an outcomes approach to evaluating community health initiatives. She and her colleagues developed a needs assessment methodology, using a participatory action research approach, to identify the community needs of Americans with disabilities called the Concerns Report Method. This methodology has been used as a tool for action and replicated with multiple diverse populations. She is a Fellow of the American Psychological Association.

Gary W. Harper, PhD, MPH, is Associate Professor in the Department of Psychology at DePaul University in Chicago. He is Program Director of DePaul University's Clinical-Community Doctoral Training Program, Co-Director of the University's Center for Community and Organization Development, and recently served as Chair of the American Psychological Association's Committee on Psychology and AIDS. The primary focus of Dr. Harper's research, evaluation, and action-oriented community work is on examining HIV sexual risk and protective factors among various groups of young people who are marginalized in society (e.g., gay/bisexual youth, urban ethnic-minority youth) and developing culturally and developmentally appropriate community-based prevention programs for these young people. In his work, he also examines the formation and maintenance of community-university partnerships, and the use of empowerment evaluation with community agencies. Dr. Harper is currently a member of the Adolescent Medicine Leadership

Group for the National Institutes of Health's Adolescent Medicine Trials Network (ATN) for HIV/AIDS Interventions, a group that is responsible for the definition and development of national research agendas related to adolescents and HIV. Within the ATN, he is currently directing an evaluation of the formation and maintenance of community-researcher partnerships across 15 communities in the mainland United States and Puerto Rico that are being formed to improve HIV prevention services for underserved youth. Dr. Harper is a Fellow of the American Psychological Association and the Society for Community Research and Action.

Community-Based Approaches to Empowerment and Participatory Evaluation

Yolanda Suarez-Balcazar

University of Illinois at Chicago

Gary W. Harper

DePaul University

KEYWORDS. Collaboration, community organizations, empowerment and participatory evaluation

Empowerment and participatory approaches to evaluation are gaining momentum in the field of community psychology (see Fawcett et al., 1996; Fetterman, 2002; Fetterman, 2001; Fetterman, Kaftarian, & Wandersman, 1996; Suarez-Balcazar & Orellana-Damacela, 1999; Wandersman, 1999;

The authors wish to acknowledge the valuable input offered by those who served as reviewers for this volume, including: Shira Benhorin, Radhika Chimata, Beth Cooper, Mimi Doll, Joseph Durlak, Brigida Hernandez, Omar Jamil, Bernadette Sanchez and Jennifer Steiner. In addition, they wish to thank their academic departments for support during the development of this volume: the Department of Occupational Therapy at the University of Illinois at Chicago and the Department of Psychology at DePaul University, as well as the editor-in-chief, Joseph Ferrari, for his guidance and support.

[Haworth co-indexing entry note]: "Community-Based Approaches to Empowerment and Participatory Evaluation." Suarez-Balcazar, Yolanda, and Gary W. Harper. Co-published simultaneously in *Journal of Prevention & Intervention in the Community* (The Haworth Press, Inc.) Vol. 26, No. 2, 2003, pp. 1-4; and: *Empowerment and Participatory Evaluation of Community Interventions: Multiple Benefits* (ed: Yolanda Suarez-Balcazar, and Gary W. Harper) The Haworth Press, Inc., 2003, pp. 1-4. Single or multiple copies of this article are available for a fee from The Haworth Document Delivery Service [1-800-HAWORTH, 9:00 a.m. - 5:00 p.m. (EST). E-mail address: docdelivery@haworthpress.com].

Wandersman et al., 2004). As community evaluators and researchers we find ourselves learning from our communities every time we engage in empowerment and participatory evaluation. Since the publication of Fetterman et al.'s (1996) book on the topic, *Empowerment Evaluation* has become an essential approach to evaluation that is consistent with the principles of community psychology, but not much research has been published or presented regarding its utility.

Empowerment evaluation is rooted in *Empowerment Theory* (see Zimmerman, 2000; Fawcett et al., 1994). According to Fetterman (1996), "empowerment evaluation is the use of evaluation concepts, techniques, and findings to foster improvements and self-determination" (p. 4). The evaluation process is designed to increase different stakeholders' capacity to conduct their own evaluation and to increase the control of actions taken to improve program impact (Wandersman et al., 2004).

Although empowerment evaluation is in itself participatory, not all participatory evaluations are empowering since they do not always focus on the transfer of skills and the building of evaluation capacity (see Flaspohler, Wandersman, Keener, Maxwell, Ace, Andrews, and Holmes). Participatory evaluation is rooted in *Participatory Action Research (PAR)* (see Jason, Keys, Suarez-Balcazar, Taylor, Davis, Durlak & Isenberg, 2004; Selener, 1997), an approach that highlights not only the active participation of stakeholders in the evaluation process, but also a sharing of control related to critical decisions. Although PAR has been utilized in other fields such as sociology for a number of years, community psychologists are becoming increasingly aware of the applications of this methodology when conducting program evaluations with communities. Both of these approaches, empowerment and participatory evaluation, are particularly beneficial when working with communities that have experienced varying degrees of marginalization and oppression, as they offer community members a true voice in the evaluation process and provide them with new resources (see Harper, Contreras, Bangi, & Pedraza).

In empowerment and participatory evaluation, the evaluator and community partner may assume different roles throughout the collaborative process (e.g., coach, educator, provider of technical assistance, etc.). As evaluators, though, we need to be mindful of the inherent power that we possess when partnering with community members since community agencies are often in need of evaluation assistance for program improvement and sustainability, and frequently do not have the skills or resources to conduct such evaluations independently. Thus we should be accountable to these communities by joining in solidarity with them and attempting to share our skills (Nelson, Prilleltensky, & MacGillivary, 2001). The cases illustrated in this volume are examples of sharing knowledge through evaluation. They also demonstrate that the end value of empowerment and participatory evaluation is not the report itself, but a continuous process of program improvement and capacity building.

This volume includes an array of articles on varying aspects of empowerment and participatory evaluation, ranging from theoretical models to empirical investigations to case studies. Three papers present broad frameworks, phases and tools for empowerment and participatory evaluation, on which the emphasis is transferring skills and building capacity, and demonstrate the ways in which these models have been applied to evaluation projects within a range of communities (see Fawcett, Boothroyd, Schultz, Francisco, Carson, & Bremby; Flaspohler, Wandersman, Keener, Maxwell, Ace, Andrews, & Holmes; Suarez-Balcazar, Orellana-Damacela, Portillo, Sharma, & Lanum). The other three papers illustrate specific efforts to implement empowerment and participatory evaluation with a range of stakeholders and highlight the ways in which community members collaborated with evaluators and were actively engaged in the evaluation process (see Benee & Garrard; Harper, Contreras, Bangi, & Pedraza; Sharma, Suarez-Balcazar, & Baetke). All six articles highlight benefits and impacts of the approach taken in partnership with various stakeholders. As researchers we need to pay special attention to the benefits that participatory and empowerment procedures are bringing to our community partners and the organizations and people they represent.

REFERENCES

Fawcett, S. B., Paine-Andrews, A., Francisco, V. T., Schultz, J. A., Richter, K. P., Lewis, R. K. et al. (1996). Empowering community health initiatives through evaluation. In D. Fetterman, S. Kaftarian, & A. Wandersman (Eds.), *Empowerment evaluation: Knowledge and tools for self-assessment and accountability* (pp. 256-276). Thousand Oaks, CA: Sage.

Fawcett, S. B., White, G. W., Balcazar, F. E., Suarez-Balcazar, Y., Mathews, R. M., Paine-Andrews, A. et al. (1994). A contextual-behavioral model of empowerment: Case studies involving people with physical disabilities. *American Journal of Community Psychology, 22,* 471-496.

Fetterman, D. M. (1996). Empowerment Evaluation: An introduction to theory and practice. In D. Fetterman, S. Kaftarian, & A. Wandersman (Eds.), *Empowerment evaluation: Knowledge and tools for self-assessment and accountability* (pp. 3-46). Thousand Oaks, CA: Sage.

Fetterman, D. M. (2001). *Foundations of Empowerment Evaluation.* Thousand Oaks, London: Sage Publications, Inc.

Fetterman, D. M. (2002). Empowerment Evaluation: Building communities of practice and a culture of learning. *American Journal of Community Psychology, 30,* 89-102.

Fetterman, D. M., Kaftarian, S. & Wandersman, A. (Eds.). (1996). *Empowerment evaluation: Knowledge and tools for self-assessment and accountability.* Thousand Oaks, CA: Sage.

Jason, L., Keys, C., Suarez-Balcazar, Y., Taylor, R.R., Davis, M., Durlak, J., & Isenberg, D. (2004). *Participatory Community Research: Theories and Methods in Action.* Washington, DC: American Psychological Association.

Nelson, G., Prilleltensky, I., & MacGillivary, H. (2001). Building value-based partnerships: Toward solidarity with oppressed groups. *American Journal of Community Psychology, 29,* 649-677.

Selener, D. (1997). *Participatory action research and social change.* Ithaca, NY: Cornell Participatory Action Research Network.

Suarez-Balcazar, Y., & Orellana-Damacela, L. (1999). A university-community partnership for empowerment evaluation in a community housing organization. *Sociological Practice: A Journal of Clinical and Applied Research, 1,* 115-132.

Wandersman, A. (1999). Framing the evaluation of health and human services programs in community settings: Assessing progress. *New Directions for Evaluation, 83,* 95-102.

Wandersman, A., Keener, D. C., Snell-Johns, J., Miller, R.L., Flaspohler, P., Livet-Dye, M., Mendez, J., Behrens, T., Bolson, B. & Robinson, L. (2004). Empowerment Evaluation: Principles and Action. In L. Jason, C. Keys, Y. Suarez-Balcazar, R. R. Taylor, M. Davis, J. Durlak, & D. Isenberg (2004). *Participatory Community Research: Theories and Methods in Action.* Washington, DC: American Psychological Association.

Zimmerman, M. A. (2001). Empowerment theory: Psychological, organizational and community level of analysis. In J. Rappaport & E. Seidman (Eds.), *Handbook of Community Psychology* (pp. 43-63). New York: Plenum.

Implementing an Outcomes Model in the Participatory Evaluation of Community Initiatives

Yolanda Suarez-Balcazar

University of Illinois at Chicago

Lucía Orellana-Damacela
Nelson Portillo
Aparna Sharma
Mindy Lanum

Loyola University Chicago

SUMMARY. Community-based organizations (CBOs) face a number of challenges in conducting evaluations of their initiatives. This paper illustrates some of the processes and challenges that arose in our efforts to collaborate with eight CBOs to implement an outcomes model adapted from the United Way model (1996) to evaluate their initiatives using a participatory approach. The outcomes model emphasizes the link be-

---

This project was funded in part by a grant from BP Social Global Investment to Loyola University Center for Urban Research and Learning and the Department of Psychology.

Address correspondence to: Yolanda Suarez-Balcazar, PhD, Department of Occupational Therapy (MC 811), College of Applied Health Sciences, Chicago, IL 60612 (E-mail: *ysuarez@uic.edu*).

[Haworth co-indexing entry note]: "Implementing an Outcomes Model in the Participatory Evaluation of Community Initiatives." Suarez-Balcazar, Yolanda et al. Co-published simultaneously in *Journal of Prevention & Intervention in the Community* (The Haworth Press, Inc.) Vol. 26, No. 2, 2003, pp. 5-20; and: *Empowerment and Participatory Evaluation of Community Interventions: Multiple Benefits* (ed: Yolanda Suarez-Balcazar, and Gary W. Harper) The Haworth Press, Inc., 2003, pp. 5-20. Single or multiple copies of this article are available for a fee from The Haworth Document Delivery Service [1-800-HAWORTH, 9:00 a.m. - 5:00 p.m. (EST). E-mail address: docdelivery@haworthpress.com].

10.1300/J005v26n02_02

tween program goals, activities, outputs (process evaluation) and outcomes. An empowerment and participatory approach to evaluation emphasizes self-determination and evaluation skills building. We illustrate challenges and alternative solutions as we implemented our evaluation process comprising five phases: developing the partnership and planning the evaluation; developing an outcomes logic model; identifying the methodology and data collection strategies; interpreting and reporting findings; and utilization of findings. Overall, our collective experience indicates that despite some challenges, staff gained important evaluation skills and produced information useful to improve programs. *[Article copies available for a fee from The Haworth Document Delivery Service: 1-800-HAWORTH. E-mail address: <docdelivery@haworthpress.com> Website: <http://www.HaworthPress.com> © 2003 by The Haworth Press, Inc. All rights reserved.]*

KEYWORDS. Outcomes model, community partnerships for participatory evaluation

INTRODUCTION

   Community-based organizations (CBOs) deem the evaluation of their initiatives both as a necessity and as a challenge (Connell & Kubisch, 1998; Cousins, Donohue, & Bloom, 1996). It is currently widespread among funding agencies to make financial support of community programs contingent on evaluation of such initiatives. In fact, United Way has made it obligatory for all the agencies receiving funding to implement their outcomes measurement system for continuation of support. Finding the appropriate measurement tools and specifying the right indicators can be an overwhelming job for staff who experience case overload, high turnover and low-paying jobs (Flora & Grosso, 1999). The purpose of this paper is to discuss the process of implementing an outcomes model with eight CBOs in a large midwestern city to evaluate their initiatives using a participatory and empowerment approach. This discussion begins with an introduction of the project, the conceptual model used along with a description of the evaluation phases. The phases comprise: developing a university-community partnership and planning the evaluation; developing an outcomes model; selecting the methodology and data collection procedures; interpreting and reporting research findings; and utilizing findings. For each of these phases, we describe process issues, discuss challenges in the implementation process and discuss alternative solutions to address the challenges.

The community-based organizations participating in this project were selected by the funding agency. These organizations were sponsoring a number of community initiatives, including violence prevention programs; job referral and job training for minority young adults; tutoring and mentoring programs for inner city youth; and a parent training program.

Outcomes Model and Evaluation Theory

Outcomes Model

A number of outcome models, also referred to as program logic models, have been proposed in the comprehensive community initiatives evaluation literature. Among these frameworks are: the United Way of America (1996) Outcomes Measurement model; Milstein and Chapel (2002) Model of Change; Linney and Wandersman (1996) Prevention Plus Model; and Connell and Kubisch (1998) and Weiss (1995) Theory of Change Approach.

The outcomes model proposed by United Way of America (1996) highlights the connection between program goals, inputs, activities, outputs and outcomes. Within this model, program goals are specific statements of who the target population is and what the program is intended to achieve; inputs are defined as program resources and context. Activities and outputs include the program components and strategies that take place. This documentation of program activities and program implementation is defined as process evaluation (see Linney & Wandersman, 1996), while outcome evaluation involves measuring changes in participants' knowledge, skills and behaviors, and/or attitudes; or changes in community conditions.

Evaluation Theory

A participatory and empowerment approach to evaluation is rooted in Participatory Action and Research (Selener, 1997) and empowerment theory (Zimmerman, 2000). According to Fetterman (1996), "Empowerment evaluation is the use of evaluation concepts, techniques, and findings to foster improvements and self-determination" (p. 4). The evaluation process is designed to increase the staff's evaluation capacity so that staff from CBOs can document the process and impact of their programs (Fetterman, Kaftarian, & Wandersman, 1996). The end value of evaluation is not the report itself but a continuous process of program improvement (Fawcett et al., 1996). Within this participatory and empowerment approach, CBO staff share responsibilities with the university partners, are involved throughout the process, and are seen as experts with respect to community issues. The evaluation process emphasizes program development, implementation and improvement, and the power and decision-making resides with the community partners (Fetterman et al., 1996). The evaluation research then becomes a genuinely collaborative process with an emphasis on improving program services and practices (Fawcett et al., 1996).

THE PROCESS OF IMPLEMENTING AN OUTCOMES MODEL: EVALUATION PHASES

The overall outcomes model used in this project is an adaptation of the model proposed by United Way (1996). What follows is a description of the phases implemented by the researchers using an adaptation of Fawcett et al. (1996) and Suarez-Balcazar and Orellana-Damacela (1999). We will discuss challenges and alternatives to address such challenges.

Phase I: Developing a Partnership and Planning the Evaluation

In a participatory approach, researchers and community members must work together to understand social issues particularly relevant to them and develop viable solutions (Suarez-Balcazar, Davis, Ferrari et al., 2004). Conducting evaluation using this approach implies involvement of community partners throughout the entire research process (Suarez-Balcazar & Orellana-Damacela, 1999). The collaborative partnerships for this project were developed based on key principles of trust, mutual respect, and acknowledgement of the organizational culture (Nelson, Prillentensky, & MacGillivary, 2001; Suarez-Balcazar et al., 2004). The principal investigator and one graduate student (one graduate student was assigned to each of the CBO involved) made the first contact to the CBO who had already received a letter from the funding agency and the university team about the project. The university research team met with the staff and executive directors to learn about the

CBO, toured the community, reviewed archival materials, and learned about the agency's program, the organizational culture, and previous evaluation experiences. Furthermore, all expectations and partnership's goals were clarified early in the process. These facilitated the development of a trustful relationship and helped us also in identifying the evaluation needs of each CBO. The key contact staff, appointed by the executive director, and graduate students had weekly meetings about the project, while community leaders provided feedback and assistance on a monthly basis. During the early meetings, we clarified roles and expectations of the community and university partners; shared values and principles of a participatory approach to implementing an outcomes model; and identified the specific program to be evaluated.

Several planning sessions were conducted at each organization in which partners discussed the program to be evaluated, previous attempts at evaluating the program, and evaluation questions of interest to different stakeholders.

Challenges and Potential Solutions

One of the most frequent challenges we faced during this phase was staff turnover. By the time the university team had developed a strong relationship with a staff member and designed an evaluation plan (i.e., goals and expectations), the key contact had left the organization and a new staff came to the team. In fact, in three of the eight organizations our key contact staff left the organization before finishing the project. High staff turnover typical of CBO may impact the potential strength of the collaborative relationship with the CBO, therefore we find it critical to developing a strong collaborative relationship with more than one staff member from the onset of the project and have different stakeholders involved in the process. Having more than one staff also facilitates the transferring of evaluation skills to other agency staff. Often it is not feasible for the organization to assign more than one community contact as the key partner because of staff overload. It is imperative then, that the partnership team (composed of both university and community representatives) keeps all relevant stakeholders such as the executive director, community leaders, and program staff involved and up-to-date on the evaluation process.

Another challenge often encountered is the mystification of evaluation. We found that fears about evaluation were common. These included fear that the program will be at risk and that staff performance will be questioned; fear of losing control of the program; and the belief that evaluation is difficult and cumbersome (see Posavac & Carey, 1997). In addition, many of the CBO staff we worked with believed that their initiatives were effective and beneficial to the community and that evaluation was not necessary (see Schorr, 1997). Wandersman et al. (2004) suggest careful attention to discussing stakeholders concerns and myths. Taking the time to clarify myths, concerns, and planning the evaluation is critical to building the collaborative partnership and building ownership over the evaluation process. Often, when the CBO is not ready to engage in the evaluation process, it is necessary to conduct strategic planning to clarify program goals and objectives.

Phase II: Developing an Outcomes Model

Engaging in a discussion about the program itself fosters critical thinking and self-determination (Fetterman et al., 1996). This is accomplished through a process of outcomes brainstorming sessions, in which an outcomes logic model linking program goals, resources and activities, outputs, outcomes and impact is developed (United Way, 1996). These sessions are also intended to explore methods that allow for systematic documentation of indicators of program success (e.g., changes in participants' knowledge, skills and attitudes). The participating CBO staff described these brainstorming sessions as a luxury due to the limited opportunities that CBO staff has to reflect about their own programs. One staff member said, "In seven years that I have been in this organization, this is the first time we have sat down to reflect about what we are doing and what we would like to accomplish." In our brainstorming sessions, we try to include all program stakeholders including program developers, implementers, coordinators and a community-consumer representative.

Challenges and Potential Solutions

During these brainstorming sessions, much of the CBO's internal politics and conflicts of interest surfaced. While the staff of the majority of the participating CBOs shared somewhat clear and common assumptions about program expectations, we had to mediate internal organizational conflicts to achieve consensus in two separate CBOs. In addition, CBOs found it difficult to modify their common practice of measuring and reporting outputs only. Community-based programs are used to report outputs such as number of people served, workshops conducted, etc., but not necessarily outcomes, and often find it challenging to identify specific indicators of changes as they relate to participants' skill/competencies, knowledge and attitudes.

To deal with the above challenge we moved into outcomes brainstorming only after a strong relationship had been established with the agency partners, after clarifying roles and expectations, partnership goals and careful planning. However, as outside researchers, it is sometimes impossible to avoid internal politics and conflict of interest within the CBO (Fawcett et al., 1996). When we come into a CBO, we are often unaware of the agency culture and politics. That is why we recommend coming into the university-community partnership ready to learn from CBO staff about the history and culture of the organization and the community it serves. Setting the stage for a partnership in which both partners, the university and community, are ready to exchange resources and knowledge and learn from each other is one of the core principles of our field.

Phase III: Identifying the Methodology and Data Collection

Advocates of empowerment and participatory evaluation have called for the use of both qualitative and quantitative methods (Fetterman et al., 1996) and the unit of analysis to include the individual and community conditions (Hollister & Hill, 1995). We endorse the use of both methodologies. For the most part, the CBOs we worked with were sensitive to the selection of methodology and appreciated our multimethod approach. Most of the CBOs had previously conducted listening sessions or focus groups, satisfaction questionnaires, and a few CBOs had previously completed an analysis of community conditions. The CBO staff also appreciated the fact that all the stakeholders, service users, were included in the brainstorming sessions and in the development of methodology. Three of the eight CBOs had done evaluations in the past and already had a set of evaluation measures that included surveys, behavioral checklists, and tracking systems that they wanted to refine with our assistance. Whether we assisted in the development of a new tool or helped refine an existing tool, the measures were adapted to reflect the outcomes yielded from the brainstorming sessions and the environmental and cultural context of the program being evaluated. We were also careful in allowing the involved stakeholders to take ownership over the development of tools and protocols to increase likelihood of future use and adoption by the CBO.

Challenges and Potential Solutions in Developing Tools and Protocols

Some of the challenges we experienced included finding existing tools and tracking systems that the CBOs could use to measure outcome indicators. Finding an existing tool that was both methodologically sound and relevant to the CBOs' programmatic goals was often time intensive. Once the tool was refined or developed, it also became a challenge to incorporate multiple stakeholders perspectives and needs (e.g., service user vs. funding director).

One way to deal with the challenge of finding or developing the right indicators and evaluation tools was to move to this phase only after the development of an outcomes logic model in which the evaluation team develops a record of resources by documenting current resources and strategies being used. In addition, we assisted with the review of existing literature on the topic, and reviewed how other programs in other communities were tracking similar outcomes. To address the issue of diverse perspectives, one strategy that worked for us was to go over the instruments and tools as a group and not on an individual basis. In this way, staff members, other stakeholders and researchers were able to consider and discuss each other's suggestions. This made it easier for the partnership team to incorporate everyone's comments.

Challenges and Solutions in Selecting the Data Collection Method and Its Implementation

The selection of a methodology is dependent upon the program to be evaluated and the population being served and this can vary from agency to agency. In one CBO, we assisted the staff in conducting an evaluation of overall services in which they wanted to assess the perspective of community residents. Once a tool was developed, the challenge for us was choosing the most culturally sensitive way of collecting data (see Marín, 1993). The staff believed that Latino/a residents would not respond to mail surveys, phone interviews, or attend group assessments. At a planning and brainstorming session, it was determined by the staff that the assessment could be accomplished by a random door-to-door canvassing with community-university dyads. This dyad approach allowed the data collection to remain methodologically rigorous while facilitating the entry of non-community members. Consistent with a participatory approach, data collection was conducted in such a way as to increase the sense of involvement for agency staff and community volunteers. Together, the university-community partnership team considered issues, such as the optimal times and days to interview residents (weekend mid-mornings), safety concerns, and potential language barriers (one dyad member must be bilingual). Using this methodology, the community assessment survey response rate was high and the reception by residents was very positive.

Phase IV: Interpreting and Reporting Findings

Integrating and communicating findings in participatory and empowerment research efforts are relevant tasks for the community researcher because findings represent potential tools for social change and action (Fawcett et al., 1996). Dalton, Elias, and Wandersman (2001) consider effective communication of findings imperative, given its potential impact on community members and CBOs' subsequent actions in their communities. However, working together with CBO staff and diverse stakeholders in interpreting and reporting findings can present some challenges (Harper & Salina, 2000).

Challenges and Potential Solutions

One of the most challenging steps for CBO staff was the actual analysis of data and interpretations of findings. For the most part the university partner(s) provided training and coaching during this phase and in a couple of CBOs, staff members had the skills to do it with minimal instruction. We need to make sure that tools and protocols used to measure relevant indicators can be adopted by the staff and implemented regularly without necessarily the researchers assistance.

In addition, interpreting and communicating evaluation findings constitute complex processes when implementing an outcomes logic model for an evaluation of community initiatives. Given that decisions about how to improve the program depend on what the evaluation results show, potential conflicts are likely to arise when deciding what to report and how to report it (Posavac & Carey, 1997). Harper and Salina (2000) have asserted that the process of data analysis and interpretation should be a collective task and include different stakeholders. The particular challenge of the partnership team included providing information to stakeholders with different information needs, viewpoints, and extents of involvement in the process.

Our approach in this project consisted of writing the report in collaboration with key community partners, discussing the results with a variety of stakeholders, even those who were not invested in the process, and distributing copies of preliminary reports to obtain feedback from different stakeholders. Feedback received from the CBOs indicated the importance of providing short reports with visual aids and graphs, and recommendations that were clear, specific, and action-oriented.

Riley (1997) points out that higher citizen involvement and greater receptivity to people's voices constitute very effective antidotes to counteracting the university-community information gap. Our specific approach was to share data results in public forums and focus groups using an open dialogue with different community members and participants. This practice has been successfully implemented in other evaluation partnership (Suarez-Balcazar & Orellana-Damacela, 1999) and is highly recommended when information needs to be communicated to community groups (Hampton, Francisco, & Berkowitz, 1993).

Phase V: Utilization of Evaluation Findings

Maximizing the use of evaluation information is a crucial component of the outcomes model. Currently, there is an emphasis in the evaluation field on assessing the impact of the evaluation process upon the CBO (Cousins, Donohue, & Bloom, 1996). This is a reaction to the fact that evaluation results have sometimes been ignored by stakeholders (Mayer, 1996; Weiss, 1995). Several authors have reported that participatory and empowerment approaches to evaluation increase the likelihood of the stakeholders using the information generated by the evaluation. This increase occurs due to a bust in: (a) their sense of ownership of the evaluation; (b) their credibility and trust in the process, and (c) a more thorough cognitive processing of the information (Cousins & Earl, 1995; Wandersman et al., 2004).

The model that we are describing focuses on utilization at every step of the evaluation process. At the beginning of the partnership, the stakeholders were asked to define ways in which they would use the evaluation information. During the planning and data collection, stakeholders were included in the decision-making and were kept informed of the preliminary information that was being generated. In this way, they could reflect on the meaning of the findings and how it would affect their program. When producing the final report, stakeholders were asked to provide feedback and were informed of the final results. In some CBOs, key partners co-author the final report with the researchers. These activities provided further opportunities for them to have their viewpoints discussed and included, and increase their sense of ownership of the information provided. Finally, at the end of the process, stakeholders were interviewed and asked to report events of utilization of the evaluation information.

Leviton and Hughes (1981) suggest three categories of utilization: instrumental, conceptual, and symbolic. Instrumental use implies that evaluation information is used for decision making or problem-solving purposes. It means making small or fundamental changes in the community initiative, practices, or policies that affect the program itself. Conceptual use refers to the influence that the evaluation process and results exert on stakeholders' attitudes, beliefs and opinions about the program being evaluated. Symbolic or persuasive use makes reference to the evaluation information being used to advocate for issues and persuade people to act on a determined way (Johnson, 1998).

One example illustrating the three types of utilization involved a participating CBO that provided a parenting program. Two program coordinators met with our team to discuss the implementation of the recommendations from the study. Parents called for a more dynamic series of talks, increased interaction, and counseling from staff, among other recommendations. The staff engaged in some changes in practices and services in terms of how they were delivering the program. After implementing changes in practices and services, such as hiring a new counselor (instrumental use), the staff met with the partnership team again to obtain feedback, and indicated that they had acquired a more comprehensive view about their program due to the discussion sessions with the partnership team and the information from the evaluation process (conceptual use). In this same CBO, the partnership team was invited to discuss the findings of the evaluation project with the organization's board of directors. As a result of this meeting, the board made changes in funding allocation (symbolic use) that facilitated the implementation of some of the evaluation recommendations (instrumental use).

Challenges and Potential Solutions

There were challenges associated with compiling information on CBO staff utilization of evaluation findings. The first challenge was the high staff turnover in the participating CBOs. Often the staff member with whom the evaluation process was initiated had left the agency before the evaluation report was produced. This affected the transferring of skills and utilization of findings to impact program. The new staff members had somewhat different expectations about how to use the information and different opinions regarding the usefulness of the evaluation findings. The partnership team needs to be prepared for new staff members or other stakeholders to participate intermittently throughout the process. However, having different key contacts throughout the process can impact negatively the transfer of capacity for evaluation. The partnership team needs to address this issue and discuss the importance of consistency of contact.

TIME SPENT IN PROCESS-RELATED ISSUES

We consider it important to provide some information about the time involved in conducting participatory evaluation in collaboration with CBOs. Table 1 illustrates the number of hours invested in each of the evaluation phases. The partnership team spent an average 13 hours in the first phase, including developing the relationship and planning the evaluation. The organization in which we spent the most hours was the one with the internal conflicts and lack of readiness to engage in the process. The average time spent in the second phase, outcomes brainstorming, was eight hours. This was affected by the complexity of the program to be evaluated, the number of staff members involved in the process, and the level of agreement about program goals. During the methodology phase the partnership team spent an average of 45 hours. This phase involves developing/refining instruments and tracking systems, data collection and analyses. The next phase, reporting findings, revealed an average of eight hours. The final phase utilization yielded an average of seven hours. The amount of time depicted on the table was distributed across 16 months. The partnership team kept time sheets on a weekly basis to report to the project coordinator.

DISCUSSION

This paper illustrates some relevant issues in the form of challenges and solutions in our efforts to implement an outcomes model using an empowerment and participatory approach to evaluation. Although the list of challenges we reviewed is by no means exhaustive, we mentioned those most commonly found when implementing an outcomes model with CBOs.

TABLE 1. Estimated Number of Hours Spent in Process Issues Across Phases

Type of Community Initiative	Phase I	Phase II	Phase III	Phase IV	Phase V	Total of Hours
Community Health Center[a]	6	9	42	6	6	65
Job Referral Services[b]	8	7	21	6	6	44
Job Training[b]	13	7	82	15	7	124
Parent-Training[b]	6	7	16	6	12	45
Violence Prevention[b]	22	13	42	10	10	92
Youth Leadership[a]	18	7	68	10	6	105
Youth Mentoring and Tutoring[a]	9	7	25	6	4	51
Youth Service[b]	24	10	64	4	8	110
Totals	106	67	360	63	59	636

Notes: Numbers do not reflect time spent doing literature review, reviewing documents and archival information. Description of the phases is as follows: Phase I: Developing a partnership and planning the evaluation; Phase II: Developing an outcomes logic model; Phase III: Identifying the methodology and data collection; Phase IV: Interpreting and reporting findings; Phase V: Utilization and maximizing the use of evaluation findings. Subscript *a* indicates sites with only one key contact. Subscript *b* indicates sites with two or more key contacts.

The implementation of the outcomes model and empowerment approach resulted in many benefits for the CBOs and the university partners in the evaluation team. In general, CBO staff praised the fact that they had been listened to and kept informed throughout the evaluation process and many at the end of the process felt more comfortable planning their own evaluation. Furthermore, three of the sites expressed interest in maintaining contact with the university team to assist them in further implementation of the model. Three graduate students, who were part of the evaluation team, were offered internships at these sites to continue the partnership. In fact, our experience has shown that a participatory and empowerment approach to evaluation increases the likelihood of ownership of the process, adoption of evaluation methods and tools, and increases utilization of evaluation findings (see Wandersman et al., 2004). Furthermore, we observed that CBO staff who were more involved in the process developed more ownership, evaluation skills and took the findings more seriously acting upon them. Some of the comments expressed by our community partners included: "I feel more ready and prepared to do evaluation," "I now understand the importance of documenting the impact of our programs."

Many of the CBOs benefited directly by securing additional funding, including the evaluation report in grant submissions and receiving positive feedback from the board of directors. University partners also benefited from these partnerships. We learned about the diverse communities and concerns faced by the CBOs, we improved our skills to conduct action research in university-community partnerships, and also became more aware of how to deal with the challenges of conducting community research and action.

REFERENCES

Connell, J., & Kubisch, A. C. (1998). Applying a theory of change approach to the evaluation of comprehensive community initiatives: Progress, prospects, and problems. In K. Fulbright-Anderson, A.C. Kubisch, & J.P. Connell (Eds.), *New Approaches to Evaluating Community Initiatives. 2* (15-44). New York: The Aspen Institute.

Cousins, J. B., Donohue, J. J., & Bloom, G. A. (1996). Collaborative evaluation in North America: Evaluators' self-reported opinions, practices and consequences. *Evaluation Practice, 17,* 207-226.

Cousins, J. B., & Earl, L. M. (1995). The case for participatory evaluation: Theory, research, practices. In J. B. Cousins & L. Earl (Eds.), *Participatory evaluation in education: Studies in evaluation use and organizational learning* (pp. 3-17). London: Falmer.

Dalton, J. H., Elias, M. J., & Wandersman, A. (2001). *Community psychology. Linking individuals and communities.* Belmont, CA: Wadsworth/Thomson Learning.

Fawcett, S. B., Paine-Andrews, A., Francisco, V. T., Schultz, J. A., Richter, K. P., Lewis, R. K. et al. (1996). Empowering community health initiatives through evaluation. In D. Fetterman, S. Kaftarian, & A. Wandersman (Eds.), *Empowerment evaluation: Knowledge and tools for self-assessment and accountability* (pp. 256-276). Thousand Oaks, CA: Sage.

Fetterman, D. (1996). Empowerment evaluation: An introduction to theory and practice. In D. Fetterman, S. Kaftarian, & A. Wandersman (Eds.), *Empowerment evaluation: Knowledge and tools for self-assessment and accountability.* Thousand Oaks, CA: Sage.

Fetterman, D., Kaftarian, S., & Wandersman, A. (Eds.). (1996). *Empowerment evaluation: Knowledge and tools for self-assessment and accountability.* Thousand Oaks, CA: Sage.

Flora, C., & Grosso, C. (1999). Mapping work and outcomes: Participatory evaluation of the farm preservation advocacy network. *Sociological Practice: A Journal of Clinical and Applied Sociology, I*(2), 133-155.

Hampton, C., Francisco, V. T., & Berkowitz, B. (1993). Communicating information to funders for support and accountability. *Community Tool Box*, Part J, Ch. 39, Sect. 4 [on-line]. Available: *http://ctb.lsi.ukans.edu/tools*.

Harper, G. W., & Salina, D. D. (2000). Building collaborative partnerships to improve community-based HIV prevention research: The university-CBO collaborative partnership (UCCP) model. *Journal of Prevention & Intervention in the Community, 19*, 1-20.

Hollister, R. G. & Hill, J. (1995). Problems in the evaluation of community-wide initiatives. In J. Connell & colleagues (Eds.). *New Approaches to Evaluating Community Initiatives: Concepts, Methods, & Contexts.* Washington, DC: The Aspen Institute.

Johnson, R. B. (1998). Toward a theoretical model of evaluation utilization. *Evaluation and Program Planning, 21*, 93-110.

Leviton, L., & Hughes, E. (1981). Research on the utilization of evaluation. A review and synthesis. *Evaluation Review, 5*, 525-548.

Linney, J. A. & Wandersman, A. (1996). Empowering community groups with evaluation skills: The prevention plus III model. In D. Fetterman, S. Kaftarian, & A. Wandersman (Eds.), *Empowerment evaluation: Knowledge and tools for self-assessment and accountability* (pp. 256-276). Thousand Oaks, CA: Sage.

Marin, G. (1993). Defining culturally appropriate community interventions: Latino/as as a case study. *Journal of Community Psychology, 21*, 149-161.

Mayer, S.E. (1996). Building community capacity with evaluation activities that empower. In D. Fetterman, S. Kaftarian, & A. Wandersman (Eds.), *Empowerment evaluation: Knowledge and tools for self-assessment and accountability* (pp. 256-276). Thousand Oaks, CA: Sage.

Milstein, B., & Chapel, T. (2002). Developing a logic model or theory of change. *Community Tool Box*, chapter 2: section 7. Retrieved from *http://ctb.ku.edu/tools/EN/chapter_1002.htm.*

Nelson, G., Prilleltensky, I., MacGillivary, H. (2001). Building value-based partnerships: Toward solidarity with oppressed groups. *American Journal of Community Psychology, 29*, 649-677.

Posavac, E. J. & Carey, R. G. (1997). *Program evaluation methods and case studies.* Upper Saddle River, NJ: Prentice Hall.

Riley, D. A. (1997). Using local research to change 100 communities for children and families. *American Psychologist, 52*, 424-433.

Schorr, L. (1997). *Common purpose: Strengthening families and neighborhoods to rebuild America.* New York: Anchor Books.

Selener, D. (1997). *Participatory action research and social change.* Ithaca, NY: Cornell Participatory Action Research Network.

Suarez-Balcazar, Y., & Orellana-Damacela, L. (1999). A university-community partnership for empowerment evaluation in a community housing organization. *Sociological Practice: A Journal of Clinical and Applied Research, 1*, 115-132.

Suarez-Balcazar, Y., Davis, M., Ferrari, J., Nyden, P., Olson, B., Alvarez, J., Molloy, P., & Toro, P. (2004). University-community partnerships: A framework and an exemplar. In L. Jason, K. Keys, Y. Suarez-Balcazar, M. Davis, J. Durlak, & D. Isenberg. *Participatory Community Research: Theories and Methods in Action.* Washington, DC: American Psychological Association.

United Way of America (1996). *Outcome and measurement resource network* [on-line] Available: *http://national.unitedway.org/outcomes/.*

Wandersman, A., Keener, D., Snell-Johns, J., Miller, R., Flaspohler, P., Livet-Dye, M., Mendez, J., Behrens, T., Bolson, B., & Robinson, L. (2004). Empowerment Evaluation: Principles and Action. In L. Jason, K. Keys, Y. Suarez-Balcazar, M. Davis, J.

Durlak, & D. Isenberg. (2004) *Participatory Community Research: Theories and Methods in Action*. Washington, DC: American Psychological Association.

Weiss, C. H. (1995). Nothing as practical as good theory: Exploring theory-based evaluation for comprehensive community initiatives for children and families. In J.P. Connell, A. Kubisch, L. Schorr, & C. H. Weiss (Eds.), *New approaches to evaluating community initiatives: Concepts, methods, and contexts* (pp. 65-92). Washington, DC: The Aspen Institute.

Zimmerman, M.A. (2000). Empowerment theory: Psychological, organizational and community level of analysis. In J. Rappaport & E. Seidman (Eds.), *Handbook of community psychology* (pp. 43-63). New York: Plenum.

Building Capacity
for Participatory Evaluation
Within Community Initiatives

Stephen B. Fawcett
Renée Boothroyd
Jerry A. Schultz
Vincent T. Francisco
Valorie Carson
Roderick Bremby

University of Kansas

SUMMARY. Participatory evaluation is the process by which those doing the work contribute to understanding and improving it. In the context

The authors deeply appreciate the contributions of their many colleagues in community initiatives, support organizations, and grantmaking institutions who have taught them about this work. These include KU Work Group colleagues who contributed to this manuscript, including John Cyprus, Paul Evensen, Jacquie Fisher, Larissa McKenna, and Adrienne Paine-Andrews. They also thank colleagues at participating state and community initiatives, including Andrew O'Donovan of the Kansas Social and Rehabilitative Services' Office of Prevention; Kathy Smith of the Missouri Primary Care Association and the Kansas City Chronic Disease Coalition; Bobbie Berkowitz and Bud Nicola of National Turning Point at the University of Washington; and local colleagues in the School-Community initiative to prevent adolescent pregnancy. Work on which this summary report was based was funded by grants from the Robert Wood Johnson Foundation, the Kansas Health Foundation, the Kansas Office of Social and Rehabilitative Services, the Ewing Marion Kauffman Foundation, and the U.S. Centers for Disease Control and Prevention.

[Haworth co-indexing entry note]: "Building Capacity for Participatory Evaluation Within Community Initiatives." Fawcett, Stephen B. et al. Co-published simultaneously in *Journal of Prevention & Intervention in the Community* (The Haworth Press, Inc.) Vol. 26, No. 2, 2003, pp. 21-36; and: *Empowerment and Participatory Evaluation of Community Interventions: Multiple Benefits* (ed: Yolanda Suarez-Balcazar, and Gary W. Harper) The Haworth Press, Inc., 2003, pp. 21-36. Single or multiple copies of this article are available for a fee from The Haworth Document Delivery Service [1-800-HAWORTH, 9:00 a.m. - 5:00 p.m. (EST). E-mail address: docdelivery@haworthpress.com].

10.1300/J005v26n02_03

of community initiatives, this often involves co-production of knowledge–local people and outside evaluators sharing responsibility for gathering data and interpreting its meaning. We outline a six-component framework for participatory evaluation: (a) Naming and framing the problem/goal to be addressed, (b) Developing a logic model (or theory of practice) for how to achieve success, (c) Identifying evaluation questions and appropriate methods, (d) Documenting the intervention and its effects, (e) Making sense of the data, and (f) Using the information to celebrate and make adjustments. Incorporating examples from different community initiatives, we examine how to support and build capacity for participatory evaluation. To help guide the collaborative work of participatory evaluation among community members and outside evaluators, we outline orienting questions (e.g., what are we seeing?) and core activities (e.g., characterizing the data) for each component, and describe Internet-based supports to help reflect and act on what we see. Finally, we discuss challenges, benefits, and opportunities in this approach to supporting and building capacity for participatory evaluation within community initiatives for health and development. *[Article copies available for a fee from The Haworth Document Delivery Service: 1-800-HAWORTH. E-mail address: <docdelivery@haworthpress.com> Website: <http://www.HaworthPress.com> © 2003 by The Haworth Press, Inc. All rights reserved.]*

KEYWORDS. Capacity building, community initiatives, logic model, community change

Community work–local people coming together to address an issue that matters to them–is sometimes seen as too "untidy" a context for formal research and evaluation. It is often complex, evolving, and dynamic. A community initiative is likely to include multiple and interrelated components. For example, social marketing, support, and celebration activities may be part of an effort to promote caring engagements among adults and youth. A community's intervention efforts are likely to unfold gradually over time. For example, a community intervention to improve school readiness might begin with a public information effort to encourage parents to read to their children, and later, introduce a new mobile library program and other related efforts. When barriers are encountered or new opportunities emerge, the planned intervention may be adjusted to reflect what is feasible and timely. To understand the complexity of such adaptive systems (Eoyang, 1997), investigators must be close to the gradual unfolding of interventions throughout the life span of community initiatives.

In participatory evaluation, local people and outside researchers share evaluation responsibilities in pursuit of both understanding and improvement (Fawcett et al., 1996). By contrast, traditional evaluation approaches often rely on "outside experts," such as consultants or university-based researchers, often at a distance from what is happening. The involvement of local community experts facilitates access to local knowledge and experience, making the inquiry's questions and methods relevant to local needs and customs. In collaboration, the involvement of outside experts facilitates access to established and innovative methods to enable broader support and accountability to outside audiences such as grant makers. Working together, local people and outside researchers share in setting the research agenda, gathering information, making sense of it, and using information to celebrate and make adjustments.

Participatory evaluation engages local practitioners from the initial design of the research project through determination of its final conclusions. This emphasis on the involvement of local people is shared by other fields of inquiry such as participatory action research (Whyte, 1991; Green et al., 1995), empowerment evaluation (Fawcett et al., 1996; Fetterman, Kaftarian, & Wandersman, 1996), community-based participatory research (Fawcett, Schultz, Carson, Renault, & Francisco, 2002; Minkler, 2000; Minkler & Wallerstein, in press), ethnography (Agar, 1980; Spradley, 1979), qualitative evaluation (Guba & Lincoln, 1989; Patton, 1980), and action anthropology (Stull & Schensul, 1987). As such, participatory evaluation refers to the process by which those involved in the work contribute to understanding about it– and to applying that knowledge to improve the effort.

This manuscript examines the process by which local people and outside researchers share responsibility for understanding and making improvements in community initiatives. Using illustrations from actual community initiatives, we outline participatory evaluation activities within a six-component framework. We describe how Internet-based resources can support co-learning and adjustments in the process of participatory evaluation. Finally, we discuss challenges, benefits, and opportunities for the work of supporting and building capacity for participatory evaluation within community initiatives.

FRAMEWORK AND SUPPORTS FOR PARTICIPATORY EVALUATION WITHIN COMMUNITIES

Figure 1 outlines a framework and core components for the process of participatory evaluation in community initiatives. The components are interactive (i.e., mutually influencing each other), as well as iterative (i.e., repeating as necessary to incorporate needs and learning). This framework is based on the participatory approaches mentioned above, as well as the prior research and evaluation experience of the authors and other colleagues (e.g., Argyris, Putnam, & Smith, 1985; Connell, Kubisch, Schorr, & Weiss, 1995; Fawcett et al., 1996; Fawcett, Francisco, Hyra et al., 2000; Fawcett et al., 2001; Rootman et al., 2001). This section outlines activities and case examples organized within the typical unfolding of the framework.

FIGURE 1. A Framework for the Process of Participatory Evaluation in Community Initiatives

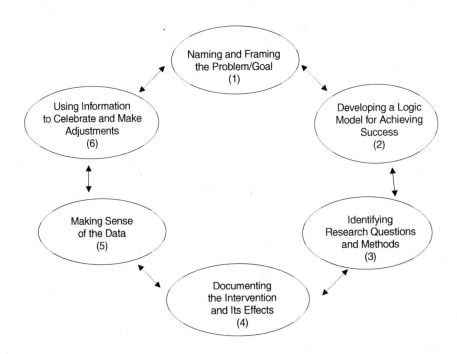

Naming and Framing the Problem or Goal

"What issue are we trying to address?" Problem setting–giving a name to the problem or goal and a framework for how to address it–may be the single most important research activity (Argyris, Putnam, & Smith, 1985; Schon, 1983) since it determines where we look to understand and take action. When we name a problem or goal, we focus on the behaviors and key actors that are critical to addressing it. For example, when a community group names its goal as "increasing caring engagements among adults and children," it focuses attention on the behaviors, such as talking with children or providing support, of key actors including parents and neighbors. In participatory evaluation, all those with something to gain or lose work together to develop a shared vision and mission. By reviewing community concerns and identifying available assets, communities can focus their efforts on features of the issue that can yield improvement.

Case example of support and capacity building for the work. Consider Connect Kansas, a statewide effort to improve outcomes for children and youth led by the Office of Prevention of the Kansas Department of Social and Rehabilitative Services (SRS). To support naming and framing the work of Connect Kansas, we facilitated dialogues among key stakeholders about their common objectives and shared vision. The group agreed upon the Kansas Health Foundation's vision–"In the next 20 years, Kansas will become the best state in the nation to raise a child"–and Connect Kansas's nine developmental outcomes, such as "safe and supportive communities" and "youth choose healthy behaviors." These were used to help orient the state's shared work to improve outcomes for Kansas's children and youth. This group also worked together to gather and review data to identify shared indicators of success.

To help build capacity for Connect Kansas's efforts in participating communities throughout the state, we developed a customized and Internet-based Workstation. This "Connect Kansas Workstation" used the capabilities of a comprehensive online resource, the *Community Tool Box* (*http://ctb.ku.edu/*) (Fawcett, Schultz, Carson, Renault, & Francisco, 2002) for building capacity, documentation and evaluation, and co-learning and adjustments. It offered how-to information to participating communities and support organizations for planning and implementing the work (e.g., frame the issue; develop vision and mission statements; identify community assets). We also offered a televised course on "Building Healthy Communities" that used information in the *Community Tool Box* to help plan and structure dialogues about the work (e.g., building coalitions and partnerships, developing strategic plans, evaluating local efforts). It provided opportunities for supported practice and reflection among those doing, funding, and supporting the work. The course enhanced the core competencies of those involved, which, in turn, extended their ability to conduct these key activities.

Developing a Logic Model for Achieving Success

"How will we get from here to there?" A logic model (Marsh, 1998; Milstein & Chapel, 2002) describes the sequence of events for bringing about change related to the chosen problem or goal, and provides a picture of how to get from "here," the current conditions, to "there," the vision for success. It may use bi-directional arrows between elements, such as between intervention and outcome, to highlight presumed, but as yet undemonstrated, relationships. Figure 1, with its interrelated circles, provides a simple logic model or roadmap for the process of participatory evaluation. Similarly, a generalized logic model for the work of building healthy communities might use a roadmap to depict: (a) collaborative planning, (b) community action and intervention, (c) facilitating community and systems change, and (d) improvements in population-level behavior change and related outcomes (Fawcett, Francisco, Hyra et al., 2000).

Evaluators and community leaders share responsibilities to describe candidate pathways from where we are now, as revealed by community assessments, to where we want to be, agreed-upon improvements in the community-level outcomes that define success. The logic model includes a description of (a) interrelated sub-outcomes, (b) environmental and community changes related to the outcome, and (c) the context and broader conditions relevant to success.

Case example of support and capacity building for the work. The Kansas City Chronic Disease Coalition (KC-CDC) is a metropolitan area-wide effort to reduce disparities in health outcomes associated with race and ethnicity. Together with staff of the Missouri Primary Care Association, we facilitated discussions in which Coalition members targeted more distant outcomes such as reduced incidence of diabetes and cardiovascular diseases. The group developed sub-outcomes, such as increased physical activity or having a diet lower in fat, and considered local conditions such as a history of discrimination and cultural and first-language diversity that may influence health disparities. Next, we helped facilitate action-planning workshops in which Coalition members identified community and systems changes to be sought to address risk and protective factors. For example, Coalition representatives of inner-city clinics and other Coalition partners agreed to provide additional information about health consequences, increase access to preventive health services, and create opportunities for peer support for healthy behaviors. Finally, together we reviewed a "picture" of the emerging logic model to get feedback on whether it fit their sense of the collaborative work.

The resulting logic model developed by KC-CDC had five interactive and iterative steps including: (a) Collaborative planning and capacity building (process), (b) Community action and intervention (outputs), (c) Community and systems change such as new or enhanced programs, policies or practices (intermediate outcomes), (d) Widespread behavior change, including increased physical activity and lower fat diet (more distant outcome), and (e) Reduced disparities in health outcomes such as cardiovascular diseases (more distant outcome) (Fawcett, Carson, Collie, Bremby, & Raymer, 2000). Learning modules and other practical guidance, such as for identifying risk and protective factors, found in the online Workstation provided supports for refining and using the logic model without the presence of outside researchers or consultants.

Identifying Research Questions and Appropriate Methods

"What do we want to know and how will we know it?" A research question frames what is to be examined in the inquiry. It is grounded in the logic model and has implications for how success is defined. A research question focuses on the hypothesized relationships among different elements. For example, the bi-directional arrow between community and systems change and widespread behavior change might suggest a research question such as, "Under what conditions are community and systems changes associated with widespread behavior change?" Evaluation questions reflect what key stakeholders want to understand; and the research methods must fit the questions, interests, and available resources.

To develop research questions and select appropriate methods, the community (and outside) evaluation team must clarify the purpose of the evaluation and interests of the end users. For example, a community group might decide to focus on promoting peace in the neighborhood as their primary purpose. A particular interest might be to change the environment, such as by limiting access to weapons and alcohol, to effect widespread behavior change related to homicide and injury. Research methods, such as qualitative interviews and behavioral surveys, must stand the test of accuracy (i.e., reliability), sensitivity (i.e., validity), feasibility (i.e., practicality), and utility (i.e., guiding improvement).

Case example of support and capacity building for the work. We worked closely with the KC-CDC to frame evaluation questions consistent with their logic model for reducing disparities in health outcomes associated with race and ethnicity. We proposed two core evaluation questions: (1) "Does the initiative bring about community and systems change related to the mission of reducing disparities?" and (2) "Under what conditions are community and systems changes related to improvements in widespread behavior change (e.g., in physical activity and diet) and more distant health outcomes?" Together, we identified and adapted appropriate evaluation methods to document the unfolding of community and systems changes. Next, members of the Coalition examined behavioral surveys, such as the U. S. Centers for Disease Control and Prevention's Behavioral Risk Factor Surveillance System, and archival records of population-level indicators (e.g., incidence of cardiovascular diseases among different populations) that could be used to evaluate changes in more distant outcomes. Both Coalition members and KU Work Group staff used an Internet-based "Kansas City Chronic Disease Coalition's Workstation." This support tool–including online help in "developing an evaluation plan"–made the work of finding and using research methods easier and more rewarding.

Documenting the Intervention and Its Effects

"What are we doing? Is it making a difference?" Documentation captures the activities and effects of the initiative as they unfold. For example, a community initiative to promote childhood immunizations might be engaged in documenting new or modified: (a) programs, such as a social marketing effort with new parents, (b) policies, such as requiring parents and guardians to provide evidence of child immunization as a condition for receiving other benefits, and (c) practices, such as health care providers offering immunizations in conjunction with other visits related to the mission (Francisco, Paine, & Fawcett, 1993). Community participation in documentation enables local people to play an active role in examining progress, seeing early markers of success, and ensuring accountability to grantmakers and local constituents.

Community members and outside researchers share responsibilities for determining and tracking data to be collected. This input helps to frame a system for data collection and reporting that is responsive to the interests of key stakeholders such as community leaders and grantmakers. In addition, community members are actively involved in data gathering and recording to help detect the unfolding of the intervention and evaluate its effects on behavior and outcome indicators of success. Collaborative engagement of community partners and outside researchers in ongoing evaluation and documentation efforts supports their role as co-managers of, and co-experts in, assessing progress.

Case example of support and capacity building for the work. Consider the National Turning Point initiative funded by the Robert Wood Johnson Foundation for public health improvement in twenty-two state health departments (Schultz, Fawcett, Francisco & Berkowitz, 2003). KU Work Group and Turning Point's staff worked together to refine a protocol for measuring systems change and analyzing its contribution to public health improvement. A pilot test with several state health departments helped refine documentation and analysis methods.

First, the National Program Office and KU Work Group helped orient state health department staff to the task of documenting systems changes for public health improvement (e.g., Fawcett et al., 1995; Francisco, Paine, & Fawcett, 1993). Second, state staff became primary data entry persons and began to score events based on the shared system for measurement. Third, we provided online supports for data entry, including prompts for critical information and online help systems with reminders of definitions and scoring instructions. Fourth, the participating states and National Program Office staff shaped consistent and reliable scoring of their data by reviewing together the entered data and giving and responding to feedback on the scoring of systems changes. Finally, National Program Office staff helped link the documentation activities to their emerging evaluation questions, such as "Are the initiatives facilitating systems change related to public health improvement?" and "How are they contributing to the ten essential public health services?"

A customized "Public Health Improvement Work Station" for this initiative made documentation easier and more rewarding by offering online capabilities to: (a) document community and systems change, (b) display trends and discontinuities in rates of change, (c) analyze the contribution of community and system changes using visual analyses such as pie charts showing the distribution of systems changes among the ten essential public health services, (d) clarify success and make adjustments through use of an online Troubleshooting Guide, (e) capture success stories, and (f) generate and review online and print reports of accomplishments to make accountability easier.

Making Sense of the Data

"What are we seeing? What does it mean?" The involvement of community members and outside researchers in participatory evaluation generates shared understanding about what is happening. Evaluation of a comprehensive initiative to improve caring for older adults might focus sense-making on determining possible relationships among changes in the environment with improvements in behaviors, or more distant community-level outcomes. For instance, local evaluators of a home visitor program checking on elderly neighbors might examine increases in caring engagements and their impact on indicators of independent living and well-being of older adults. Collaboration in characterizing and reflecting on the meaning of the data helps join the specialized knowledge of outside researchers with the experiential knowledge of local people.

Community members and outside researchers work together to examine how an intervention addresses the problem or goal, contributes to changes in behavior and outcome data trends, and fulfills its stated purpose. Community members and outside evaluators look for patterns in the unfolding of the intervention and its effects to identify potentially important components of the approach. The focus is on discontinuities, marked increases or decreases, in rates of key measures, such as community or systems change, and events or factors associated with them, such as changes in leadership or completion of an action plan. For instance, a consistent relationship between "action planning" (i.e., identifying particular changes in programs, policies and practices to be sought) and accelerated rates of community change has been documented in the literature (Roussos & Fawcett, 2000).

Case example of support and capacity building for the work. In collaboration with representatives of the Kansas Health Foundation's School-Community initiative to reduce risk for adolescent pregnancy (Paine-Andrews et al., 1999), KU Work Group staff helped make sense of this initiative's efforts by linking community constituents to resources that enabled them to more easily see what was occurring. Internet-based supports through a "School-Community Workstation" based on the *Community Tool Box* helped frame and model critical thinking about the data, characterize emerging patterns, and evaluate current progress.

Community initiatives worked with KU Work Group staff to review progress quarterly through one-page narratives, examples, and graphs of rates of community and systems changes. These regular dialogues provided opportunities for critical reflection about "What are we seeing?" and "What does it mean?" Working together, staff of the initiatives and the KU Work Group gathered feedback from expert and community constituents and incorporated it into updates and adjustments in project action plans. With prompting, initiative staff explored the contribution of the unfolding intervention to better understand its potential effects on behavior, such as abstinence and unprotected sexual activity, as well as community-level indicators, in particular, estimated pregnancy rates for 15-19-year-old female adolescents. Much of this sense-making was facilitated by the customized School-Community Workstation and its abilities to (a) generate real-time graphs to display trends and discontinuities in rates of change, (b) depict and analyze the contribution of community changes, such as pie charts showing the distribution of community changes focused in the school sector rather than in businesses or government, and (c) facilitating sense-making and adjustments through a troubleshooting guide that includes reflection questions, such as "Are you facing resistance or opposition?," and links to helpful sections in the *Community Tool Box* such as "Responding to Opposition."

Using the Information to Celebrate and Make Adjustments

"What do we do now, and how?" Community engagement in participatory evaluation enables initiatives to address accountability, celebrate successes, and use their data to improve efforts. For example, a community initiative to increase affordable housing might use evidence of change to honor and reenergize those who contributed, and to refocus efforts in needed areas. In participatory evaluation, members of community organzations and outside evaluators collaborate to use data as evidence. Data, such as high and sustained rates of community and systems change, and positive feedback from key constituents, offer evidence of current progress and help to sustain focus and momentum. Communicating data and lessons learned to relevant audiences can help community initiatives to redirect energies, address priority areas and challenges, and obtain additional resources and commitments to sustain the initiative. Working together, community initiatives and outside evaluation teams attempt to understand what works and the conditions under which they work (Roussos & Fawcett, 2000). In turn, they use this information to help make improvements and secure support for sustaining successful efforts.

Case example of support and capacity building for the work. In the School-Community initiative, KU Work Group staff collaborated with initiative staff to offer a number of support activities to help build capacity in the three participating communities. First, the KU Work Group helped develop skills for using the data by preparing models of oral presentations of the initiative's accomplishments that were adapted by participating communities. Second, staff of the initiatives created events to celebrate and award accomplishments using tips on conducting honoring ceremonies found in the *Community Tool Box*. Third, the KU Work Group and local staff shared opportunities such as retreats on lessons learned, joint presentations at professional conferences, and co-authorship of manuscripts to reflect on and disseminate information about what works. Fourth, together, we framed data analyses to address shared evaluation questions and specific audiences such as "How are we contributing to the community's efforts to reduce adolescent pregnancy and promote adolescent health?" Fifth, we outlined and integrated data findings and implications into communications for key stakeholders such as reports to local Advisory Boards and to grantmakers supporting the initiative. Sixth, KU Work Group and community initiative staff incorporated recommendations for adjustments into efforts for continuous improvement such as revisions in the initiative's action plan or the reports prepared by the KU Work Group. Finally, we used features of the customized online Workstation, such as the *Community Tool Box* Troubleshooting Guide for "Evaluation, Sensemaking, and Improvement," to help make the work of adjustment easier and more rewarding.

CHALLENGES AND BENEFITS OF PARTICIPATORY EVALUATION

Amidst a growing appreciation for the value of participatory evaluation within community initiatives, attempts to support and build capacity for this work have been challenging. First, both local people and outside researchers may lack knowledge, skills, and other resources to document the unfolding intervention or interpret findings in a political context. Second, the time and effort required for evaluation activities–along with other competing requirements–may be a barrier to collaboration. Third, distance or communication barriers may limit the contact necessary to build trust and effective working relationships. Fourth, past history of work with "outside researchers" may not have respected local knowledge, responded to local input, or contributed to the promised benefits of increased understanding and improvement of local conditions. Fifth, prevailing incentives may work against participatory evaluation. Local people may respond more to the immediate benefits of having the initiative "look good." By contrast, independent researchers may prefer "controlled studies" that maximize understanding, but limit local variation and influence. Finally, grantmakers' policies for so-called "independent" evaluation of community initiatives may inadvertently distance local people from outside researchers and limit the researcher's role to assessing merit, not contributing to improvement.

Despite these challenges, participatory evaluation is particularly valuable since local and outside people share responsibilities for the work of understanding and improving local efforts. Participatory evaluation enhances access to both the "experiential" knowledge of local people, such as what matters and why, and the "scientific" assessment about what works and under what conditions it works. As such, we may increase the relevance of evaluation questions to local interests and the fit of evaluation methods with local practices and resources. Since local people are closer to the context, they are better able to document the unfolding of the initiative and its meaning and impact. Participatory evaluation can also enhance the capacity of communities to use data for issues of accountability, celebrate successes, and improve performance and outcome. In sharing power as "co-experts," together we can make better sense of community efforts.

CONCLUSION

We can imagine future conditions to support state-of-the-art efforts to build capacity for participatory evaluation. First, formal courses, training workshops, and distance education could be used to enhance core competencies of this work. Second, new communications technology like the *Community Tool Box* could be used to make this work easier and more rewarding. Third, more opportunities to communicate this work, such as through special issues of professional journals addressing participatory evaluation, would enhance this practice. Fourth, advanced training and certification programs could help assure competence among outside researchers and local participants. Finally, philanthropic and governmental grant makers could make participatory evaluation, and evidence of enhanced capacity for it, a condition of memoranda of agreements among community initiatives and those who support and evaluate them (Fawcett, Francisco, Paine-Andrews, & Schultz, 2000).

Using illustrations from actual state and community initiatives, this manuscript makes a case for the value and potential of building capacity for participatory evaluation of community initiatives. When evaluation research activities are shared among local people and outside researchers, we enhance the quality of understanding about community initiatives and available resources for making indicated improvements. In building capacity for this work, we strengthen local and outside researchers' competence in generating knowledge and translating it into practice. By transforming conditions to support this work, we build bridges of relationship and responsibility among the once-separated communities of knowing and doing.

REFERENCES

Agar, M.H. (1980). *The professional stranger: An informal introduction to ethnography*. New York: Academic Press.

Argyris, C., Putnam, R., & Smith, D. M. (1985). *Action science*. San Francisco: Jossey-Bass Publishers.

Connell, J.P., Kubisch, A.C., Schorr, L.B., & Weiss, C.H. (1995). *New approaches to evaluating community initiatives: Concepts, methods, and contexts*. Washington, DC: The Aspen Institute.

Eoyang, G.H. (1997). *Coping with chaos: Seven simple tools*. Cheyenne, WY: Lagumo Corporation.

Fawcett, S.B., Carson, V., Collie, V., Bremby, R., & Raymer, K. (2000). *Promoting health for all: An action planning guide for improving access and eliminating disparities in community health*. Lawrence: University of Kansas, Work Group on Health Promotion and Community Development.

Fawcett, S.B., Francisco, V.T., Hyra, D., Paine-Andrews, A., Schultz, J.A., Russos, S., Fisher, J.L., & Evensen, P. (2000). Building healthy communities. In A. Tarlov and R. St. Peter (Eds.), *The society and population health reader: A state and community perspective* (pp. 75-93). New York: The New Press.

Fawcett, S.B., Francisco, V.T., Paine-Andrews, A., & Schultz, J.A. (2000). A model memorandum of collaboration: A proposal. *Public Health Reports, 115*, 174-179.

Fawcett, S.B., Paine-Andrews, A., Francisco, V.T., Schultz, J., Richter, K.P., Berkley-Patton, J., Fisher, J., Lewis, R.K., Lopez, C.M., Russos, S., Williams, E.L, Harris, K.J., & Evensen, P. (2001). Evaluating community initiatives for health and development. In I. Rootman, M. Goodstadt, D. McQueen, L. Potvin, J. Springett, & E. Ziglio (Eds.), *Evaluation in health promotion: Principles and perspectives* (pp. 241-270). Copenhagen, Denmark: World Health Organization–Europe.

Fawcett, S.B., Paine-Andrews, A., Francisco, V.T., Schultz, J., Richter, K.P., Lewis, R.K., Harris, K.J., Williams, E.L, Berkley, J.Y., Lopez, C.M., & Fisher, J.L. (1996).

Empowering community health initiatives through evaluation. In D. M. Fetterman, S.J. Kaftarian, & A. Wandersman (Eds.), *Empowerment evaluation: Knowledge and tools for self-assessment and accountability* (pp. 161-187). Thousand Oaks, CA: Sage Publications.

Fawcett, S.B., Schultz, J.A., Carson V.L., Renault, V A., & Francisco, V.T. (2002). Using Internet-based tools to build capacity for community-based research and other efforts to promote community health and development. In M. Minkler and N. Wallerstein (Eds.), *Community-based participatory research for health*. San Francisco: Jossey-Bass.

Fawcett, S.B., Sterling, T.D., Paine-Andrews, A., Harris, K.J., Francisco, V.T., Richter, K.P., Lewis, R.K., & Schmid, T.L. (1995). *Evaluating community efforts to prevent cardiovascular disease*. Atlanta, GA: Centers for Disease Control and Prevention, National Center for Chronic Disease Prevention and Health Promotion.

Fetterman, D.M., Kaftarian, S.J., & Wandersman, A. (Eds.). (1996). *Empowerment evaluation: Knowledge and tools for self-assessment and accountability*. Thousand Oaks, CA: Sage Publications.

Francisco, V.T., Paine, A.L., & Fawcett, S.B. (1993). A methodology for monitoring and evaluating community health coalitions. *Health Education Research: Theory and Practice, 8*, 403-416.

Green, L.W., George, M.A., Daniel, M., Frankish, C.J., Herbert, C.J., Bowie, W.R., & O'Neill, M. (1995). *Study of participatory research in health promotions: Review and recommendations for the development of participatory research in health promotion in Canada*. British Columbia: Institute of Health Promotion Research, The University of British Columbia.

Guba, E., & Lincoln, Y. (1989). *Fourth generation evaluation*. Newbury Park, CA: Sage.

Marsh, J. (1998). *The continuous improvement toolkit*. London: B.T. Batsford Ltd.

Milstein, B. & Chapel, T. (2002). Developing a logic model or theory of change. *Community Tool Box,* Chapter 2: Section 7. Retrieved from *http://ctb.ku.edu/tools/EN/chapter_1002.htm*.

Minkler, M. (2000). Using participatory action research to build healthy communities. *Public Health Reports, 115*, 191-197.

Minkler, M. & Wallerstein, N. (Eds.) (in press). *Community-based participatory research for health*. San Francisco: Jossey-Bass.

Paine-Andrews, A., Harris, K.J., Fisher, J.L., Lewis, R.K., Williams, E.L., Fawcett, S.B., & Vincent, M.L. (1999). Effects of a replication of a school/community model for preventing adolescent pregnancy in three Kansas communities. *Family Planning Perspectives, 31*, 182-189.

Patton, M.Q. (1980). *Qualitative evaluation methods*. Beverly Hills, CA: Sage.

Rootman, I., Goodstadt, M., McQueen, D., Potvin, L., Springett, J. & Ziglio, E. (Eds.). (2001). *Evaluation in health promotion: Principles and perspectives*. Copenhagen, Denmark: World Health Organization–Europe.

Roussos, S.T. & Fawcett, S.B. (2000). A review of collaborative partnerships as a strategy for improving community health. *Annual Review of Public Health, 21*, 369-402.

Schon, D.A. (1983). *The reflective practitioner: How professionals think in action.* New York: Basic Books.

Schultz, J.A., Fawcett, S.B., Francisco, V.T., & Berkowitz, B. (2003). Using information systems to build capacity: The Public Health Improvement Tool Box. In P. O'Carroll, W.A. Yasnoff, M.E. Ward, R. Rubin, & L. Ripp (Eds.), *Public health informatics and information systems: A contributed work.* New York: Springer-Verlag.

Spradley, J.P. (1979). *The Ethnographic Interview.* New York: Holt, Rinehart, & Winston.

Stull, D., & Schensul, J. (1987). *Collaborative research and social change: Applied anthropology in action.* Boulder, CO: Westview.

Whyte, W.F. (Ed). (1991). *Participatory action research.* Newbury Park, CA: Sage Publications.

Promoting Program Success and Fulfilling Accountability Requirements in a Statewide Community-Based Initiative: Challenges, Progress, and Lessons Learned

Paul Flaspohler
Abraham Wandersman
Dana Keener
Kathryn North Maxwell
April Ace

University of South Carolina

Arlene Andrews

Institute for Families in Society, University of South Carolina

Baron Holmes

South Carolina Budget and Control Board

Address correspondence to: Abraham Wandersman, Department of Psychology, University of South Carolina, Columbia, SC 29208 (E-mail: *Wandersman@sc.edu*)

The authors would like to acknowledge and express gratitude to the members of the PIE Team who contributed to developing and implementing the accountability system across South Carolina: Cynthia Flynn, Jeffrey Sheldon, Mary Payson, Chris Volf, Floy Work, Kevin Swick, Tammy Pawloski, Lindsey Stillman, and Elizabeth "Nikki" Rash. They would also like to thank Pam Imm, Laurie Ford, Matthew Chinman, Cindy Crusto, and Joy Kaufman for significant contributions to the development of the PIE tools and processes.

[Haworth co-indexing entry note]: "Promoting Program Success and Fulfilling Accountability Requirements in a Statewide Community-Based Initiative: Challenges, Progress, and Lessons Learned." Flaspohler, Paul et al. Co-published simultaneously in *Journal of Prevention & Intervention in the Community* (The Haworth Press, Inc.) Vol. 26, No. 2, 2003, pp. 37-52; and: *Empowerment and Participatory Evaluation of Community Interventions: Multiple Benefits* (ed: Yolanda Suarez-Balcazar, and Gary W. Harper) The Haworth Press, Inc., 2003, pp. 37-52. Single or multiple copies of this article are available for a fee from The Haworth Document Delivery Service [1-800-HAWORTH, 9:00 a.m. - 5:00 p.m. (EST). E-mail address: docdelivery@haworthpress.com].

SUMMARY. Large community initiatives are a growing phenomenon both in the U.S. and worldwide. These initiatives address a wide variety of issues, including early childhood development, by integrating institutions such as schools, health agencies, and faith-based institutions that focus on separate but related aspects of community concern. A major challenge facing these initiatives is the competing demands of developing organizational capacity to promote effective programming while simultaneously delivering demonstrable results and accountability. Empowerment evaluation (Fetterman, Kaftarian, & Wandersman, 1996) is an approach to evaluation and organizational capacity building that equips participants at all levels of an organization to pursue programming quality and results. This article describes and presents lessons learned from the development and implementation of a system of tools and processes, grounded in the principles of empowerment evaluation, designed to promote quality in the planning, implementation, and evaluation of a statewide school readiness initiative. While these lessons are specifically applicable to community-based early childhood development initiatives, they are broadly applicable to initiatives fostering systems change through community development. *[Article copies available for a fee from The Haworth Document Delivery Service: 1-800-HAWORTH. E-mail address: <docdelivery@haworthpress.com> Website: <http://www.HaworthPress.com> © 2003 by The Haworth Press, Inc. All rights reserved.]*

KEYWORDS. Empowerment, program evaluation, school readiness, early childhood

INTRODUCTION

Both building capacity *and* achieving results are explicit goals of large-scale, community-based initiatives. However, tension arises when demand for results precedes building sufficient capacity to achieve results. Evaluation efforts must grapple with this tension and other unique challenges associated with the complexity of large-scale, community-based initiatives. This article describes the design, implementation, and evolution of a system of tools and processes developed to fulfill internal accountability requirements of a statewide, community-based initiative targeting school readiness. Based on the concepts of empowerment evaluation (Fetterman, Kaftarian, & Wandersman, 1996), the internal accountability system was designed to promote quality in the planning, implementation, and evaluation of each program of the initiative. Lessons learned and suggestions for future practice presented in this article are specifically applicable to community-based early childhood development initiatives and are broadly applicable to initiatives fostering systems change through community development.

Large-scale community-based initiatives[1] are a growing phenomenon both in the United States and worldwide. These initiatives have addressed a wide variety of issues (e.g., early childhood development, substance abuse prevention) by integrating institutions such as schools, health agencies, and faith-based institutions focusing on separate but related aspects of community concern. Comprehensive initiatives pursue ambitious goals through multi-agency coordination and collaboration, organizational change and the use of effective interventions. Ultimately, traditional, categorical approaches to service delivery are replaced by systems and initiatives that promote linkages across community resources.

Comprehensive community initiatives are grounded fundamentally in the belief that local problems are best addressed through local solutions (Andrews, 2003). Embedded in this relatively simple belief is the complex notion of fundamental transformation of communities and services by advancing a process of sustained improvement of individuals and organizations (Aspen Roundtable, 1997, 2002). Although the concept of comprehensive community change is not new, the last two decades have witnessed renewed interest in the use of community development as a mechanism to foster social change. This reemergence is attributed to the convergence of several trends including recognition of fragmented nature of social services and the emerging prioritization of prevention (Kubisch, Weiss, Schorr, & Connell, 1995).

A simultaneous trend in innovative programming and initiatives involves targeting early childhood as a means of promoting positive outcomes (Boyer, 1993). Advances in neurobiological, behavioral, and social sciences have increased attention on early childhood as an optimal point of intervention for the promotion of health and well-being (Committee on Integrating the Science of Early Childhood Development, 2000). Having all children enter school "ready to learn" has become a cornerstone of many political platforms and a driving force in new services (No Child Left Behind Act, 2002). A number of states including California, Florida, and North Carolina have implemented initiatives aiming to increase the availability of high quality childcare and education, improve children's health, and provide education and services to families. These statewide early childhood development initiatives share common objectives related to the national readiness goals: children having access to quality preschool programs, children receiving quality nutrition and health care, and parents having access to training and support needed to help children learn (National Education Goals Panel, 1991).

Relatively little information is available concerning whether comprehensive community initiatives are succeeding, how well initiatives are working, or how to modify them to improve their impact (Aspen Roundtable, 1997, 2002). There is also a paucity of integrated information about what works to improve school readiness through statewide initiatives (National Governors Association, 2000). Community-based initiatives and early childhood initiatives face increasing pressure from state and federal legislatures (e.g., Government Performance and Results Act, 1993) to evaluate and demonstrate evidence of tangible results. Policymakers and funders require evidence that their resources are used efficiently and are effective. In addition to formal requirements, there are several compelling reasons for evaluation: (1) evaluation methods can assist service providers in developing quality service plans, (2) ongoing evaluation helps guide adjustment of program elements, management, and future planning, and (3) dissemination of evaluation methods and results helps inform future efforts. In other words, these initiatives are accountable to those who provide resources and to those they serve and employ.

Few states have created and/or implemented integrated evaluation systems of statewide school readiness initiatives, although several are considering and developing designs for such systems (Ace & Stamper, 2000). Large community-based initiatives and initiatives targeting early childhood development present unique challenges to researchers and evaluators attempting to develop accountability systems.

Challenges to Evaluation

By definition, comprehensive community initiatives consist of a range of strategies at the individual, community, and policy level; may be directed at multiple outcomes; and are carried out in uncontrolled community settings (Aspen Roundtable, 1997, 2002). The structures of these initiatives are inherently complex, making it difficult to isolate variables and identify effective elements (Brown, 1995). An evaluation must deal with the "parts" (i.e., individual programs) and the synergy of the "whole." Evaluation of several programs, which may overlap or incorporate multiple goals and strategies, can be complicated, especially if the goal of the evaluation is to establish cause and effect relationships. It is also difficult to identify changes across multiple targets (individuals, families, and communities). Additionally, evaluators must reconcile the competing expectations of diverse stakeholders without diluting or excessively complicating evaluation plans.

An additional set of challenges is associated with initiatives targeting early childhood development (National Governors Association, 2000). Lack of consensus regarding bottom line impacts (e.g., defining school readiness) and difficulty in assessing even clearly defined proximal outcomes in preschool age children (e.g., approaches to learning) complicate the task of evaluating early child development initiatives (Boyer, 1993; Knitzer & Page, 1998; Moore et al., 1999). In addition, the institutions that focus on preschool-aged children typically lack the capacity to conduct evaluations and state systems typically lack the resources to track the development of young children. Evaluation efforts face the need to develop effective systems that collect data from the bottom up.

Evaluation of community-based child development initiatives is further complicated by unrealistic expectations of funders. Legislative requirements regarding evaluation and accountability are often accompanied by unreasonable timelines (National Governors Association, 2000). Initiatives sponsored by public funds are frequently expected to present evidence of achievement soon after funding begins. An appropriate model for evaluating these initiatives must address these complexities. Empowerment evaluation provides a compelling approach for addressing many of these complexities because of its emphasis on capacity building, collaboration, and community control.

Empowerment Evaluation

Empowerment evaluation (EE; Fetterman et al., 1996) is an approach to evaluation and organizational capacity building that equips participants at all levels of an organization (consumer, worker, manager, governor, funding partner) to pursue programming quality and results. EE is defined as "the use of evaluation concepts, techniques, and findings to foster improvement and self-determination" (Fetterman, 2001). According to Wandersman (1999):

> The goal of empowerment evaluation is to improve program success. By providing program developers with tools for assessing the planning, implementation, and results of programs, program practitioners have the opportunity to improve planning, implement with quality, evaluate outcomes and develop a continuous

quality improvement system, thereby increasing the probability of achieving results. (p. 96)

EE and participatory evaluation are distinguished from traditional approaches to evaluation through collaboration between those with a stake in the program or strategy and the evaluator. EE is distinguished from participatory evaluation by the degree of control over evaluation design and use allocated to program stakeholders and the depth of participation in the evaluation process by stakeholders (Cousins & Whitmore, 1998). A set of key characteristics or principles, taken together as a whole, distinguishes EE from other approaches to evaluation. These principles include the explicit intention to influence the quality of programs, the distribution of power and control in decision-making to program stakeholders, emphasis on program planning and continuous quality improvement, focus on collaboration and capacity building, and demystification and institutionalization of evaluation concepts and methods (Wandersman et al., 2002).

Evaluation processes are designed to empower individuals and collective groups and to promote participation. Empowerment is accomplished by building capacities of program stakeholders to understand evaluation concepts and techniques, to conduct the evaluation, and to make use of information produced through evaluation (Fetterman, 2001; Wandersman et al., 2002). Evaluation information can be used for multiple purposes at multiple levels. At the program level, service providers and program coordinators can make program adjustments in quality and quantity based on information emerging from ongoing evaluation. At the organizational level, strategic or contractual commitments can be adjusted to reflect challenges, progress, and lessons learned from the evaluation. At the funding level, administrators can monitor activities and interim outcome indicators and produce reports to inform policy makers and the public.

FIRST STEPS INTERNAL ACCOUNTABILITY SYSTEM

First Steps is a results-oriented comprehensive early childhood initiative designed to ensure that children in South Carolina start first grade ready to succeed. Modeled after North Carolina's Smart Start initiative, First Steps establishes county boards to propose and implement programming according to locally prioritized problems and needs (South Carolina First Steps, 1999). Each county forms a collaborative partnership to assess local needs and propose interventions to impact school readiness. Funded programs are encouraged to use science and best practice interventions that directly influence child readiness (e.g., improve physical health, language, social and emotional well-being) or impact external factors believed to influence child readiness (e.g., health supports, parenting skills, childcare). Each county is required to report annually on progress toward interim goals, program implementation, client satisfaction, cost savings, and improvement plans.

An internal accountability system was developed to assist county boards in meeting these requirements with the explicit intention of building the evaluation capacity of local practitioners to incorporate approaches and tools of evaluation into programming. The system was designed to provide common language, tools, and processes for programming and evaluation; address multiple programmatic and evaluation needs (e.g., progress towards outcomes, quality of implementation); promote best practices in programming; and promote uniformity/comparability in evaluation of similar programs. The internal accountability system included: (1) a set of Planning-Implementation-Evaluation (PIE) tools, (2) an Effective Practice Network, and (3) evaluation coaching. The system components were designed from an empowerment evaluation framework with the goal of assisting multiple stakeholders in understanding the logic and processes of evaluation and in developing an evaluation plan with quality.

PIE Tools

The original framework for the PIE Tools and Program Accountability System was based largely on the evaluation framework articulated in *Prevention Plus III* (Linney & Wandersman, 1991). PIE is organized around a three-step assessment model: (1) Planning (identify goals and desired outcomes), (2) Implementation (process assessment), and (3) Evaluation (outcome assessment). Outcomes are defined as the immediate effects of programming (e.g., increases in parent knowledge or parenting skills) and are distinguished from impacts, defined as distal or "bottom-line" effects (e.g., rates of school readiness). The PIE system uses a set of worksheets (the PIE shell) and "model" evaluation plans for common programs (PIE prototypes).

PIE Shell. The PIE shell provides a format for documenting each step of the three-step process. During planning, PIE shell worksheets provide a framework for documenting goals and objectives, target group recruitment and selection plans, collaboration partners and strategies, and plans for process and outcome evaluations. Programs define benchmarks, make projections about the scope and effects of intended services, and develop specific expectations for programming and evaluation. The worksheets are designed to be flexible enough to account for the variation in programming proposed across the state. Yet, they are also designed with a degree of standardization that promotes aggregate reporting, within state comparisons of programs, and linkage to the external evaluation.

PIE Prototypes. Prototype evaluation plans using the PIE forms were developed for high priority programs to promote best practices in programming and uniformity in evaluation of similar programs. Prototypes provide a summary of logical best practice options for building individual evaluation plans. Prototypes were developed for several programs including pre-kindergarten early childhood education, Parents as Teachers, and childcare quality enhancement initiatives.

Effective Practice Network

A network of effective practice experts (EPEs) was created to promote compliance with the expectation that programming operate according to state-of-the-art evidence about effective practices in early childhood development. Comprised of South Carolina experts in the content areas of school readiness (health, parenting, family strengthening, early childhood education, and transportation), the EPEs developed best practice concept papers, contributed to developing prototype PIEs, reviewed county PIE plans, and guided the coaching process.

Evaluation Coaching

Each county was assigned an evaluation coach or "PIE consultant" to build bridges among the Effective Practice Experts (representing research and best practices standards) and the major stakeholders at the state, county, and program level. The primary tasks of evaluation coaches were to provide training in the principles and purposes of evaluation, to facilitate developing specific evaluation plans for each program, and to provide ongoing technical assistance in order to build evaluation capacity at the county and program levels. The evaluation coaches operated out of a university-based institute tasked with designing and implementing the program accountability system. A separate group of technical advisers (TAs), operating out of the state First Steps Office, facilitated the start-up and ongoing operations of the forty-six county boards and partnerships. Initially, plans were to coordinate closely the work of the evaluation coach and TAs to blur boundaries between programming and evaluation; however, the demands of going to scale rapidly contributed to division of efforts by the groups.

PIE in One County

The following example provides an indication of how the PIE process was put into place in one county; however, it is important to know that considerable customization occurred across counties. The reader is cautioned in drawing conclusions from the example to the state as a whole.

Palmetto County (not the real name) is a rural county with dramatic rates of adult under-education (75% of adults have high school education or less) and low per-capita income (20% below the state average). The county ranks in the bottom third in the state on several relevant indicators including children testing "not ready" for first grade and births to mothers with inadequate prenatal care. To promote readiness rates, the local First Steps board proposed five strategies in the areas of health, parent education, early education, and childcare. An evaluation coach worked with the county to build evaluation capacity and develop and monitor evaluation plans for each program. The process was carried out slowly and deliberately with comparable emphasis on process (i.e., building relationships and capacities) and product (i.e., developing evaluation plans).

Initially, the evaluation coach focused on capacity building, attending board and strategic planning meetings to give presentations and brief workshops on evaluation concepts and skills. As capacities developed, the focus of coaching shifted to developing PIEs for individual programs. PIEs were developed collaboratively among smaller groups of key stakeholders. For example, a PIE for a planned expansion of four-year-old preschool classes involved the executive director, several board members, school principals, and teachers; a PIE for a parent education program involved three staff members from the funded agency along with the executive director. Completing a PIE amounts to articulating the theory of change that underlies a given strategy (Weiss, 1995). Stakeholders make their assumptions explicit and must reach consensus about key mechanisms and anticipated results. Doing so helps to concentrate evaluation resources and capability on key aspects of the program.

During implementation and evaluation, coaches fostered a process of mutual learning among key stakeholders through collaborative analysis of data generated during and after programming. In Palmetto County, data was analyzed and reported monthly to the local board. Regular reporting fostered examination of strengths and limitations in programming and helped shape efforts to improve programming in progress and future proposals. Over a period of 14 months, five PIEs were developed and monitored for Palmetto County. These PIEs were considered invaluable by the county executive director in meeting both the internal expectations of her county board and the external demands for accountability from the state.

The accountability system was designed to make the relationship between programming and evaluation mutually reinforcing. By conducting a standardized evaluation, program practitioners have the capacity to assess progress against benchmarks and, if necessary, make adjustments to programming in order to meet their own goals. The system capitalizes on philosophical similarities between comprehensive community-based initiatives and EE and presents unique possibilities for generating knowledge about what works and why.

Challenges, Progress, and Lessons Learned

The First Steps initiative and the internal accountability system were conceptualized and designed within a different political and economic context from the one in which they were implemented. The initiative began at the beginning of a governor's term. Over the course of the initiative, the opposition party, historically less supportive of the initiative, gained control of both houses of the legislature. At the same time, the major economic downturn led to cutbacks in state funding and shifts in programming priorities. For political and economic reasons, the initiative focused intensely on local initiative development. After three years of operation, contracts for services were awarded in all forty-six counties funding more than 400 programs. Going to scale quickly helped create popular support for the initiative by allowing people in every county to benefit from funding. However, rapid implementation of the system was complicated by insufficient infrastructure to support the complex needs of the initiative.

A primary purpose of the program accountability system was to build capacity for accountability among the county partnerships so that they could perform as learning organizations. Depending on their overall organizational development and initial capacities, some county partnerships embraced the system as an essential part of their operations, but many found it cumbersome. Complete PIE plans were developed for 109 individual programs and preliminary development took place for another 75. However, before all programs could benefit from the PIE planning process, the evaluation resources and efforts were shifted to focus on meeting external evaluation requirements. PIE plans became the foundation for Program Effectiveness Reports (PERs) prepared at the request of an external evaluation team.

Despite major shifts in political and economic context and in the evaluation design, good things happened. Previously unaccountable organizations were gently nudged toward adopting more accountable practices. Service delivery was analyzed systematically and gaps in services were identified. Large cadres of people developed new capacities in understanding early childhood effective practices, working on local collaborative initiatives, and producing information for fiscal and programmatic accountability. Finally, the effort produced valuable lessons about designing and implementing evaluation systems for large scale, community-based initiatives in the areas of (1) organizational structure/systems coordination, (2) multiple stakeholders/multiple needs, and (3) evaluation readiness.

Organizational Structure/Systems Coordination

The early intention of the team was to integrate the internal evaluation system with systems monitoring, programmatic/administrative functions and financial management. However, from the perspective of counties and program providers, three distinct groups emerged: the Office of First Steps handled programmatic and administrative concerns; an out-of-state consulting group handled accounting; and a university-based research institute developed and managed the internal accountability system described in this paper. Each group had its own information needs and developed independent data collection systems and requirements. The multiple demands and incompatible nature of these systems led to confusion and resentment among counties and providers. This three-party surface structure contradicted any intention to blur boundaries between programming and evaluation. Fiscal and implementation considerations were prioritized in distribution of resources such that evaluation was marginalized. At best, the evaluation system was seen by county partnerships as an asset, at times as an obligation and at worst evaluation was ignored.

Administrative boundaries need to be blurred or eliminated so that program development and evaluation efforts can work in a complementary fashion. In future practice, we recommend integrating evaluation early in the lifecycle of the initiative during programming. Evaluation should be seen as part of the program, not as a separate operating wing of the program avoiding language that contributes to marginalizing evaluation (e.g., use the term "evaluation coach" instead of "consultant" which implies outsider). Accountability needs to be promoted early in the grant-making process integrating information systems to serve fiscal, programming, and accountability requirements. We also recommend creating synergy among functional entities throughout the organization; program experts, evaluation experts and fiduciary managers. All should use the same terminology and be knowledgeable about the needs and timelines of each group. Finally, include members of all administrative functions in regular information exchange and systems planning.

Multiple Stakeholders/Multiple Needs

The evaluation process involved numerous stakeholders including county partnership boards, program providers, state administrators, technical assistants, effective practice experts and PIE consultants. In bringing multiple stakeholders together, inconsistent ideas often emerged about the purpose of evaluation. For instance, some stakeholders emphasized the importance of the quantitative aspects of service (e.g., how many children were served) whereas others were more concerned with assessing the degree to which quality standards were met. Others were more interested in developing capacity within counties to improve the likelihood that they would achieve outcomes. Difficulties emerged when consensus about evaluation was not achieved; this was often the result of failing to acknowledge different values within a collaborative effort. As a result, attempts to address disparate interests simultaneously produced evaluation plans that were so comprehensive that they were unachievable given limited resources for evaluation. Alternatively, some evaluation plans only addressed one set of interests and failed to promote buy-in of all parties. In either case, evaluation plans were underutilized or served a perfunctory purpose (e.g., sat in a filing cabinet).

The values and interests of all stakeholders need to be acknowledged when developing evaluation plans collaboratively. In future practice, we recommend beginning by assuming that different stakeholders value different things about evaluation. Be observant of stakeholders' values, attitudes, experiences and needs associated with the evaluation process under development. Acknowledge and validate differences between stakeholders and prioritize needs as a group. Although all values and needs for evaluation may be valid, they cannot all be addressed. Evaluation needs and values can be organized into a developmental continuum that is appropriate for a given program (Chelimsky, 1997). When different needs are acknowledged, stakeholders are not left feeling discounted or marginalized. Programs that are in the early stages of development typically benefit most from evaluation that is designed for the purpose of program improvement.

Evaluation Readiness

Program staff and stakeholders demonstrated significant variability in their initial skills, knowledge and commitment to evaluation (within and across counties). Counties with high levels of both skills and commitment were observed to be the most successful in engaging in evaluation efforts. Among counties that possessed evaluation skills but were lacking in commitment, evaluation tended to be perfunctory and underutilized. In counties with commitment but lacking skills, success depended on the degree of assistance and capacity building that took place. In many cases, restraints on time and resources prohibited consultants from intervening at the level of intensity that was needed to build the evaluation capacity of counties that needed it most.

Varying degrees of skills and commitment call for differential interventions on the part of the evaluation system. In future practice, we recommend assuming that different stakeholders have different levels of evaluation capacity and commitment to evaluation. Use informal observations to assess capacity and commitment. Optimally, systematic measures of evaluation capacity and commitment should be developed and used for this purpose (e.g., Snell-Johns & Keener, 2000). Coaching style can be matched to the existing capacity and commitment of each program. Some programs require intensive technical assistance, others minimal; some groups require more encouragement and motivation to participate in the process. When assessment reveals a deficit in skills, emphasis should be placed on teaching concepts, skills and tasks related to conducting evaluation. When assessment reveals a deficit in commitment, emphasis should be placed on identifying myths and negative assumptions about evaluation, addressing those myths and assumptions, and demystifying evaluation techniques and processes. In theory, distributing control over decisions improves commitment to the evaluation process. Finally, all stakeholders, including legislators and policymakers, need to devote adequate time and sufficient resources to building evaluation capacity.

CONCLUSION

First Steps is a comprehensive early childhood initiative that aims to improve school readiness among children in South Carolina. The First Steps case is typical of many comprehensive community-based initiatives in terms of high expectations for outcomes from funders and limited resources to build capacities in programming and evaluation. Implementing and evaluating these initiatives is extremely challenging work for stakeholders at each level (e.g., funders, evaluators, administrative staff, direct service providers). We have proposed a program accountability system (PIE) that uses an empowerment evaluation orientation to build stakeholder capacity to plan, implement and evaluate their programs and thereby increase the probability of obtaining results. The system provides valuable conceptual and practical tools for promoting program success and fulfilling accountability requirements in community-based initiatives. Lessons learned from implementing this system provide valuable suggestions for improvement that will be incorporated into future applications of the system.

NOTE

1. The terms community-based initiative and Comprehensive Community Initiative (CCI) describe similar systems and are used interchangeably throughout this paper. Although the initiative described in this case study is not explicitly labeled as a CCI per se, its design is consistent with attributes of CCIs.

REFERENCES

Ace, A., & Stamper, G. (2000). *Building a Foundation of Knowledge: How Statewide Initiatives Are Evaluated*. Paper presented at the meeting of the American Evaluation Association, Honolulu, HI.

Andrews, A. B. (2003). Comprehensive Community Initiatives. In J. R. Miller & L. B. Schiamberg & R. M. Lerner (Eds.), *Human Ecology: An Encyclopedia of Children, Families, Communities, and Environments*. Santa Barbara, CA: ABC-Clio.

Aspen Roundtable. (1997). *Voices from the Field: Learning from the Early Work of Comprehensive Community Initiatives*. Washington, DC: The Aspen Institute.

Aspen Roundtable. (2002). *Voices from the Field II: Reflections on Comprehensive Community Change*. Washington, DC: The Aspen Institute.

Boyer, E. L. (1993). *Ready to Learn: A Mandate for the Nation*. Princeton, NJ: The Carnegie Foundation for the Advancement of Teaching.

Brown, P. (1995). The role of the evaluator in comprehensive community initiatives. In J. P. Connell, A. C. Kubisch, L. B. Schorr & C. H. Weiss (Eds.), *New Approaches to Evaluating Community Initiatives* (Vol. 1). Washington, DC: The Aspen Institute.

Chelimsky, E. (1997). The coming transformation in evaluation. In E. Chelimsky & W. Shadish (Eds.), *Evaluation for the 21st Century: A Handbook*. Thousand Oaks, CA: Sage Publications.

Committee on Integrating the Science of Early Childhood Development. (2000). *Neurons to Neighborhoods: The Science of Early Childhood Development*. Washington, DC: National Academy Press.

Cousins, J. B., & Whitmore, E. (1998). Framing participatory evaluation. In E. Whitmore (Ed.), *Participatory Evaluation Approaches, New Directions for Evaluation* (Vol. 80, pp. 5-23). San Francisco: Jossey Bass.

Fetterman, D. (2001). *Foundations of Empowerment Evaluation*. Thousand Oaks, CA: Sage.

Fetterman, D., Kaftarian, S., & Wandersman, A. (1996). *Empowerment Evaluation: Knowledge and Tools for Self-Assessment and Accountability*. Thousand Oaks, CA: Sage Publications.

Government Performance and Results Act of 1993, U.S. Congress, 103rd Sess. (1993).

Knitzer, J., & Page, S. (1998). *Map and track: State Initiatives for Young Children and Families*. New York, NY: National Center for Children in Poverty.

Kubisch, A. C., Weiss, C. H., Schorr, L. B., & Connell, J. P. (1995). Introduction. In J. P. Connell & A. C. Kubisch & L. B. Schorr & C. H. Weiss (Eds.), *New Approaches to Evaluating Community Initiatives* (Vol. 1). Washington, DC: The Aspen Institute.

Linney, J. A., & Wandersman, A. (1991). *Prevention Plus III: Assessing Alcohol and Other Drug Prevention Programs at the School and Community Level: A Four-Step Guide to Useful Program Assessment*. Rockville, MD: U.S. Department of Health and Human Services, Office for Substance Abuse Prevention.

Moore, K., Manlove, J., Richter, K., Halle, T., LeMenstrel, S., Zaslow, M., Greene, A. D., Mariner, C., Romano, A., & Bridges, L. (1999). *A Birth Cohort Study: Conceptual and Design Considerations and Rationale*. U. S. Department of Education: Office of Educational Research & Improvement.

National Education Goals Panel. (1991). *The National Education Goals Report: Building a Nation of Learners*. Washington, DC: Author.

National Governors Association. (2000). *Evaluating Statewide, Community-Based Initiatives for Children* (Issue Brief). Washington, DC: NGA Center for Best Practices.

No Child Left Behind Act of 2001, U.S. Congress, 107th Sess.(2002).

Snell-Johns, J., & Keener, D. (2000). *The Past and Current Evaluation Capacity of Two Community Initiatives*. Paper presented at the meeting of the American Evaluation Association, Honolulu, Hawaii.

South Carolina First Steps to School Readiness Act, 152 (1999).

Wandersman, A. (1999). Framing the evaluation of health and human service programs in community settings: Assessing progress. In J. Telfair & L. C. Leviton & J. S. Merchant (Eds.), *New Directions for Evaluation: Evaluating Health and Human Service Programs in Community Settings* (Vol. 83). American Evaluation Association: Jossey-Bass.

Wandersman, A., Keener, D., Snell-Johns, J., Flaspohler, P., Dye, M., & Mendez, J. (2002). *The Principles of Empowerment Evaluation.* Paper presented at the Second Annual Chicago Conference on Community Research: Participatory Methods, Chicago, IL.

Weiss, C. H. (1995). Nothing as practical as good theory: Exploring theory-based evaluation for comprehensive community initiatives for children and families. In J. P. Connell, A. C. Kubisch, L. B. Schorr & C. H. Weiss (Eds.), *New Approaches to Evaluating Community Initiatives* (Vol. 1). Washington, DC: The Aspen Institute.

Collaborative Process Evaluation: Enhancing Community Relevance and Cultural Appropriateness in HIV Prevention

Gary W. Harper
Richard Contreras
Audrey Bangi

DePaul University

Ana Pedraza

Project VIDA, Chicago, Illinois

SUMMARY. Process evaluations provide multiple opportunities to improve prevention and intervention programs that benefit communities experiencing oppression and marginalization. In order to thwart the negative effects of power and privilege, it is essential that collaborative partner-

Address correspondence to: Gary W. Harper, Department of Psychology, DePaul University, 2219 N. Kenmore Avenue, Chicago, IL 60614 (E-mail: *gharper@depaul.edu*).

This work was supported in part by grants from the AIDS Foundation of Chicago, the Illinois Campus Compact for Community Service, and the DePaul University Research Council. The authors would like to thank the young women and young men who have participated in Project VIDA's HIV-prevention interventions and who have taken the time to contribute to the evaluation of these programs through surveys, interviews, and focus groups.

[Haworth co-indexing entry note]: "Collaborative Process Evaluation: Enhancing Community Relevance and Cultural Appropriateness in HIV Prevention." Harper, Gary W. et al. Co-published simultaneously in *Journal of Prevention & Intervention in the Community* (The Haworth Press, Inc.) Vol. 26, No. 2, 2003, pp. 53-69; and: *Empowerment and Participatory Evaluation of Community Interventions: Multiple Benefits* (ed: Yolanda Suarez-Balcazar, and Gary W. Harper) The Haworth Press, Inc., 2003, pp. 53-69. Single or multiple copies of this article are available for a fee from The Haworth Document Delivery Service [1-800-HAWORTH, 9:00 a.m. - 5:00 p.m. (EST). E-mail address: docdelivery@haworthpress.com].

53

ships with community-based organizations (CBOs) incorporate the voices, experiences, and skills of community members. This article presents a process evaluation that was collaboratively developed and implemented by a team consisting of members from an HIV/AIDS-related CBO and a university. The process evaluation was guided by an empowerment evaluation theoretical framework and utilized elements of narrative ethnography. The methods for the evaluation were developed to ensure cultural appropriateness, community sensitivity, and scientific rigor. Modifications made to the CBO's HIV prevention programs for Latina female adolescents and gay/bisexual/questioning Latino and African-American male adolescents incorporated specific social, cultural, and environmental factors that impact HIV risk. The multiple benefits gained by those involved in the evaluation are detailed and emphasize the importance of conducting collaborative process evaluations when developing interventions for oppressed and marginalized communities. *[Article copies available for a fee from The Haworth Document Delivery Service: 1-800-HAWORTH. E-mail address: <docdelivery@ haworthpress.com> Website: <http://www.HaworthPress.com> © 2003 by The Haworth Press, Inc. All rights reserved.]*

KEYWORDS. Process evaluation, HIV prevention, collaboration, culturally appropriate

INTRODUCTION

Process evaluations are gaining increased recognition as a means through which information can be garnered regarding the delivery of services to intended populations and the nature of such services (Gottfredson, Fink, Skroban, & Gottfredson, 1997; Miller & Cassel, 2000). Process evaluations also help inform ways in which programs can be modified and better implemented in order to allocate an agency's resources more efficiently and ensure that the specific needs of the target population are truly met (Linney & Wandersman, 1991). In addition, process evaluations clarify anticipated outcome goals and criteria used in outcome evaluations that measure a program's relevance and accomplishments.

These benefits are particularly salient for prevention and intervention programs focused on communities of people who have experienced varying degrees of oppression and marginalization by mainstream society (e.g., people of color, lesbian/gay/bisexual/transgendered people). Standard programs developed for majority group individuals often require modification before they can be utilized with individuals from oppressed groups since these interventions often do not address the specific social, cultural, political, and environmental factors that lead oppressed individuals to experience negative health outcomes. In addition, members of society who are in positions of power and privilege often create negative stories and narratives about oppressed and marginalized groups of people (Nelson, Prilleltensky, & MacGillivary, 2001). These can have damaging effects through the development of stereotypes and negative habitual behaviors that become part of daily life (Rappaport, 2000). If these narratives are intentionally or unintentionally perpetuated through unmodified mainstream interventions, they may limit the exploration of new pathways that could lead to increased well-being for oppressed groups.

Evaluators can work collaboratively with oppressed groups to conduct process evaluations that will lead to new and modified interventions that provide community members with an increased choice of narratives to incorporate into their own personal life stories (Harper, Lardon, Rappaport, Bangi, Contreras, & Pedraza, 2004; Mankowski & Rappaport, 2000). By incorporating the voices of the community into the process evaluation, the community-specific limitations created by negative stereotypes and narratives, as well as potential options for future life direction, can more easily be revealed. In addition, involvement of community members in the development of the evaluation plan and methods can lead to process evaluation strategies that are more acceptable to the community, leading to increased rates of participation. In order to build collaborative partnerships with oppressed groups of people, evaluators need to spend time immersing themselves in the community and learning about the cultural, social, political, and environmental factors that impact their population of interest. Members of the collaborative team also should recognize the strengths that each person brings to the table (e.g., prior experience, knowledge, insights, skills, abilities), since this acknowledgement can help foster a sense of shared ownership for the evaluation and diminish barriers resulting from hierarchies.

COLLABORATIVE PROCESS EVALUATION

The primary focus of this article is on describing how members of an HIV/AIDS-related community-based organization (CBO) and university-based evaluators worked collaboratively to develop and implement community appropriate process evaluation methods, and the ways in which these multiple methods helped to improve the appropriateness and relevance of the CBO's HIV prevention efforts. The collaborative partnership was developed between Project VIDA, a nonprofit community-based HIV/AIDS service organization in Chicago, and a faculty member and students at DePaul University. Project VIDA wanted to evaluate two HIV prevention interventions for youth–one that had existed already for two years and one that was new. The existing program, SHERO's, was an intervention for Latina adolescents and the new program, Young Men's Program (YMP), was developed to address the HIV prevention needs of gay/bisexual/questioning (GBQ) Latino adolescents. Both programs included two primary components: (a) community outreach aimed at providing HIV prevention information and condoms to youth in community venues where they socialize (e.g., street corners, clubs, parks, etc.), and (b) an eight-week group-based HIV prevention intervention aimed at increasing their knowledge regarding a range of HIV protective skills and decreasing participation in sexual risk behaviors. Young adults, reflective of the specific group's population, served as facilitators for the sessions and community speakers served as primary presenters of program information.

Theoretical Foundations

The collaborative partners approached the process evaluation from an empowerment evaluation theoretical framework (Fetterman, 1996) and utilized a narrative ethnographic approach (Mankowski & Rappaport, 2000; Rappaport, 1995, 2000) in guiding the development of the specific methods for the evaluation. The narrative focus lead the collaborative team to work together to reveal the various common stories that are communicated in media and popular culture to describe the youth who were the focus of the interventions in a stereotyped fashion (i.e., dominant cultural narratives), the shared stories told by the youth and other community members about themselves (i.e., community narratives), and personal stories of the youth. The collaborative team was then able to use this information to help the youth modify existing narratives that promote increased participation in risky behaviors and create new narratives through the agency's revised prevention intervention (Rappaport, 1995, 2000).

The empowerment evaluation orientation supported the formation of a collaborative partnership whereby community members became active participants in all phases of the evaluation. The university team's role was one of a resource for the agency, offering skills and assistance while the agency worked collaboratively to develop their own systems of self-evaluation (Fetterman, 1996; Zimmerman, 2000). The agency, on the other hand, provided knowledge and experience in working with members of the community, which was invaluable in ensuring that the needs of the target populations were appropriately met.

Throughout the collaborative process evaluation, narratives and stories were used to describe and document the characteristics of the SHERO's and YMP programs; describe the range of clients being served by the programs; detail the various cultural, social, environmental, relational, and individual factors that influence both sexual risk and sexual health practices of young women and young GBQ men from the community; improve the delivery of HIV prevention services by modifying the current SHERO's and YMP programs; gain insight into future funding; and to improve the agency's organizational structure related to service delivery. This information was integrated into clear and coherent conceptual themes with subsequent action plans. During this collaborative process, community members received training throughout so as to have the skills and abilities to conduct this process of self-evaluation on their own.

Developing the Collaborative Partnership

In order to create a truly collaborative evaluation plan, the members of Project VIDA and the DePaul evaluation team first spent a period of time "getting to know each other." This process of developing a mutually respectful relationship between a CBO and an evaluation team prior to creating an evaluation plan or implementing the actual evaluation is critical to an empowerment evaluation agenda (Fetterman et al., 1996; Harper & Salina, 2000). It also helps to break down hierarchies that may exist between CBOs and evaluators, as CBOs may feel that evaluators are in a position of greater power given that they have the skills and knowledge related to evaluation.

Since only one of the university team members had lived in the community served by Project VIDA, and none had worked at the agency, it was critical for the university partners not only to understand and learn more about general Latino culture, but also to learn about the specific cultures of the community, the agency, the staff members, and the populations being served by the agency. The foci for this learning were on understanding the community and agency's language, norms, and physical environment, as well as each staff member's roles, responsibilities, goals, and priorities. In addition, it was important for the agency staff to learn about the skills, abilities, and roles of their new university partners, and to assess the university members' knowledge of the community and their commitment to improving services for young people. This bi-directional learning process was accomplished by participating in agency rituals (e.g., sharing food and personal stories prior to meetings), attending program activities (i.e., street/community outreach and intervention sessions), and participating in cultural events and fundraisers (for a more detailed description see Harper, Bangi, Contreras, Pedraza, Tolliver, & Vess, in press). This relationship building process helped to coalesce the collaborative team and created a mutually respectful partnership that facilitated the development of a community relevant and culturally appropriate evaluation plan.

THE EVALUATION PLAN AND METHODS

The collaborative development of the evaluation plan and the methods to be used extended over a three-month time period and involved a series of group meetings, intervention/outreach observations, sharing of written evaluation "wish lists," and ranking of evaluation priorities. When attempting to decide upon the specific objectives and goals of the evaluation, the team focused on an evaluation plan that was mutually beneficial to all parties involved and relevant to the needs of the agency and the youth in the community. The methods for the evaluation were developed to ensure community sensitivity and scientific rigor, and members of both parties implemented them. The following sections detail the areas targeted in the evaluation plan and the methods used.

Staff Members' Skill Enhancement

Several aspects of the evaluation focused on monitoring and improving the skills of the prevention program facilitators in order to increase their effectiveness in delivering the interventions. Prior to the process evaluation, staff members who facilitated prevention groups would meet with a clinical supervisor to discuss ways to improve their program delivery and group facilitation skills. One concern that staff members expressed was that because of their multiple roles and responsibilities in the agency and the time lag between program sessions and supervision meetings, they often could not recall the details of the program sessions when they met with their supervisor. Thus, the team created a semi-structured group facilitator journal that included four distinct sections (i.e., session content, group process, session problems, personal reactions) so facilitators could systematically record their reflections after each program session. The journal was then brought to clinical supervision meetings in order to more accurately and efficiently address concerns and issues that arose during the sessions. The journals not only helped improve the staff member's skills by making the best use of their clinical supervision sessions, but also provided a systematic method for documenting problem areas that arose during program sessions so these could be addressed when making modifications to the program.

Program Promotion and Outreach Monitoring

The process evaluation team implemented a number of procedures to monitor the techniques used for promoting the program and for conducting outreach activities, since, previously, no systematic data or records had been kept on such activities. A program advertisement log was developed to record the number of flyers and brochures that were distributed, as well as the location of the distribution. An outreach activity log was developed to record the number of outreach contacts completed, the number of prevention packs distributed, and the number of risk-assessments completed. This assisted supervisors in tracking the progress of the outreach workers and determining the success of recruiting participants for the group-based intervention. A CBO log also was developed to record contacts made with agencies and included specifics on the nature of the contact and potential interest in collaborating with Project VIDA.

Two logs were used to determine the effectiveness of the various program promotion and outreach strategies. A caller log was completed each time an individual contacted Project VIDA requesting information about the two prevention programs. Callers were asked how they heard about the groups, including the medium and the location, and their response was marked on a response grid. In addition, when participants came to the group-based intervention they were asked how they learned about the program and this was documented on a tracking form. These logs helped in determining the effectiveness of the various existing outreach and promotional strategies, by indicating which approaches actually resulted in referrals to the programs. As new outreach and promotional approaches were developed, the monitoring logs offered information about their utility. With this data, the agency established new, more effective approaches to outreach and no longer had to rely on anecdotal reactions.

Program Implementation

A range of techniques was used to evaluate and improve the group-based interventions, since this was the central core of both prevention programs. When creating these evaluation methods, there was a focus on assuring that the information from these activities would be utilized by the staff members to improve their skills in conducting the prevention programs and would be used by the collaborative evaluation team to modify the programs to increase their cultural, developmental, and community relevance.

Session Evaluation Forms. The process evaluation team collaboratively revised the existing session evaluation forms to improve the cultural and developmental relevancy of the wording and structure, and to delete items that did not address the agency's areas of inquiry. The forms were shortened to include only information that would be directly relevant to improving the program, and included an open-ended question to allow participants the opportunity to make recommendations for future sessions.

Focus Groups. Focus groups were conducted with participants after each eight-week intervention cycle to obtain their views regarding five areas related to the prevention programs: (a) program location (e.g., neighborhood, facility) and structure (e.g., frequency, length, time); (b) specific session format and structure (e.g., group discussion, lecture, question and answer sessions); (c) specific session content (e.g., HIV/AIDS facts, condoms, STDs); (d) community guest speaker and facilitator characteristics (e.g., age, gender, ethnicity, dress, language, professionalism, level of knowledge); and (e) overall impressions of the group (e.g., emotional reaction, connectedness). Following the focus groups, the team members who conducted them wrote thematic reports, and this feedback was presented both orally and in written format to the prevention group facilitators.

Qualitative Interviews. Individual qualitative interviews also were conducted with past program participants in order to explore their reflections on the applied utility of the programs and to offer additional information about unique stressors that currently face the target population youth so that these issues could be addressed when modifying the program. The information gained from these interviews offered unique insights into environmental and social stressors that greatly impacted the ability of the youth to protect themselves from HIV.

Non-Participant Observations. Gender-matched non-participant observers attended approximately half of the prevention sessions within each cycle and information pertaining to the specific format and structure of the sessions was recorded on a structured coding form. The form included the following sections: (1) facilitator's comfort level; (2) facilitator's connection to the group; (3) facilitator's connection to the speaker; (4) within-group dynamics; (5) group's response to the topic; (6) group's response to the community speaker; (7) group's response to the group facilitators; (8) group's overall response to the session; and (9) observer's general reactions to the session. After the session, the observers provided direct feedback to the group facilitators in a private session, and then produced a written report. The reports served as professional development tools for the group facilitators since they discussed them with their clinical supervisor, and also assisted the collaborative team with making modifications to the programs.

Audiotape Format and Structure Analyses. Prevention sessions during the process evaluation were audiotaped and were coded by trained undergraduate research assistants. A structured coding system was developed to review and dissect the sessions' format and structure. Coders listened to the audiotapes twice and used stop watches to record a different type of information each time. The first listening was focused on recording the amount of time each type of individual spoke during the session (e.g., group facilitator, community speaker, or participant). During the second listening, the coder recorded the amount of time that was spent engaging in each of the following types of intervention activities: (1) group discussion, (2) didactic/lecture activities, and (3) question and answer sessions. In addition, coders recorded whether participants or group facilitators initiated question and answer sessions. Based on these ratings, the team was able to calculate the percentage of total session time that each type of individual spoke (e.g., facilitator, community speaker, participant), as well as the percentage of time that was spent engaged in each of the three categories of learning methods. Written reports were generated from these codings that offered percentages for each of the above stated categories and were reviewed with group facilitators and the collaborative evaluation team to assist in program improvement.

Program Manualization. Another program improvement activity that was part of the evaluation plan consisted of the standardization and manualization of the group-based interventions. This was a critical component since the staff members who were running the programs were not keeping systematic records of how they were conducting the programs and since staff turnover is typically an issue for CBOs. This also was done so that when the move to outcome evaluation occurred, there would be standard procedures for conducting the interventions. Each manual was constructed to include the session overview, objectives, critical information, materials, resources/contact people, and handouts/supplemental materials.

PROGRAM CHANGES BASED ON PROCESS EVALUATION

Modifications to Both SHERO's and YMP Programs

Data from the various process evaluation techniques were reviewed on a regular basis by the collaborative team. Based on this information and the team discussions, the two prevention programs were modified in a collaborative manner to more appropriately meet the cultural, social, developmental, and community needs of the young people. In addition, the staff involved in the programs increased their skills and abilities, both in terms of running their programs and having new skills in program evaluation that could be applied to their other agency-related activities. For both programs, the outreach venues, program promotion and prevention materials, and strategies for targeting youth were modified to more appropriately reach the youth most at risk for becoming infected with HIV. Methods and approaches that were not appropriately reaching youth who were the intended target of the interventions were deleted, and those that were most effective were further refined to enhance their effectiveness.

The structure and content of the various sessions in the group-based interventions were continually modified and re-assessed throughout the process evaluation to address the changing needs of the youth. With regard to the structure, the data from the audiotape analyses indicated that a large percentage of the time during both group-based interventions was consumed by didactic/lecture activities presented by the community presenter, and that the youth were given minimal opportunities for group discussion and interaction. This was confirmed by the reports produced by the non-participant observers, who also noted negative reactions to some of the community speakers. The responses from the participants during the focus groups and on the session evaluation forms indicated that they wanted more opportunities for interaction. They also commented that some of the community speakers were not effective at conveying information to young people, and that they preferred hearing information from the group facilitators. Thus, the format of the sessions was changed to include more interactive learning activities that were conducted by the group facilitators, to increase the amount of time devoted to group discussion and interaction, and to significantly decrease the number of community speakers that presented as well as the amount of time they presented information.

The content of the sessions was changed based on information from individual interviews, focus groups, session evaluation forms, and non-participant observations. These techniques offered valuable information about the acceptability and utility of the current topics, and also offered information about new areas to address since they revealed the unique stressors that were faced by the participants. Although the group-based interventions were initially grounded in aspects of Social Cognitive Theory (e.g., peer modeling, skills training), it became clear that they could benefit from a more specific theoretical focus that would unify the sessions–one that was more directly focused on HIV risk reduction. Therefore, the AIDS Risk Reduction Model (ARRM; Catania, Kegeles, & Coates, 1990), which is one of only a handful of models designed specifically to address HIV/AIDS risk behaviors, was selected and used as a framework in making further modifications to the group-based intervention.

Another major conceptual change that occurred was to increase both group-based interventions' focus on participants' understanding and awareness of their bodies, with a specific focus on sexual health promotion. This was accomplished through sessions devoted to sexual health, and a recurrent focus in other sessions on positive and responsible sexuality for those who chose to be sexually active. This change was based on evaluation data indicating that many of the young people participating in the programs had never been exposed to accurate and affirming information about their sexual and reproductive organs/bodies. For instance, since many Latina receive the cultural message that they are to be inexperienced in sexual matters and should suppress desires to be sexual (Holland, Ramazanoglu, Sharpe, & Thomson, 1994), prior discussions about the physical maturation of their bodies and the emergence of sexual feelings as a normal part of development were either nonexistent or fairly limited for the participants. For the young GBQ men, cultural and societal messages regarding the inappropriateness and shame attached to same-gender sexual contact (Diaz, 1998) often lead these young men to conceal their sexuality from others and to avoid conversations with adult figures who could provide them with accurate and health-promoting information about their sexuality and their bodies.

Modifications Specific to the SHERO's Program

The majority of the modifications made specifically to the SHERO's program were focused on the group-based intervention. Some efforts were made to expand the geographic focus of their outreach efforts, as the agency received increased funding to serve larger numbers of young women throughout new regions of the city. Changes were also made in the promotional materials and outreach packets to reflect changes in the focus of the intervention.

In addition to the structural changes in the group-based intervention noted in the previous section, the content of several sessions was modified based on the process evaluation data. The findings indicated that four major issues impacting the sexual health of young women in the community were: (a) desires for becoming pregnant, (b) having sexual relationships with older men, (c) involvement with gangs both as gang members and as sexual partners of male gang members, and (d) discomfort discussing sexual issues and condoms with sexual partners. With regard to pregnancy, a "Pregnancy Reality" session was developed that introduced the participants to the physical, emotional, social, and financial realities of child bearing and parenting (especially single parenting) since many had unrealistic expectations with regard to the stressors associated with being a teen mother. Issues of dating and having sexual relationships with older men and gang members were addressed in a new session focused on "Dating and Relationships," and the health threats of being a gang member were addressed in an existing session on general HIV risk (e.g., exchange of blood during fights and initiation rituals).

Given that cultural issues related to sexual silence influenced the young women's comfort discussing sexual issues with their male partners, a session was added that focused on culturally sensitive ways to improve sexual assertiveness and sexual communication and included practice in these areas. An additional thematic area that influenced the modification of existing sessions and the creation of new sessions was women's empowerment and the recognition of power differentials that exist between women and men (especially in sexual relationships). Additional sessions addressed the positive characteristics embodied by significant women throughout history and Mexican-American female role models such as their mothers and grandmothers.

Modifications Specific to YMP

Since the prevention program for young GBQ men was a new program for the agency, several specific modifications were made to both the outreach and group-based components. In addition, the program expanded to include both African-American and Latino GBQ young men since it became clear that these two groups often formed friendship groups together, attended many of the same social venues in the community, were both at high risk for HIV infection, and shared many of the social, cultural, and environmental influences that increased their risk for HIV infection. The venues for conducting outreach and recruitment were continually updated, since there were not many locations where young Latino and African-American GBQ men could congregate that were safe and sustainable. New relationships were also established with other community agencies and schools in an attempt to reach new populations of GBQ youth who could benefit from the program. The outreach and recruitment materials were altered to not only reflect the incorporation of African-American youth in the program, but also to include changing terminology related to both the identity of young men who participate in same-gender sexual behavior (e.g., "down low") as well as sexual practices that present risk (e.g., "bare backing").

The structure of the YMP group-based intervention was changed based on the process evaluation data. Since many of these young men did not have a safe place where they could talk with other GBQ youth and openly discuss issues such as romantic relationships and stressors related to their sexual orientation, each session began with a "check in" period. In addition to this structural change, the program also expanded its focus beyond the standard prevention sessions to include additional workshops focused on career and personal development, and opportunities for social outings such as movie nights and trips to a local amusement park.

Several content changes were made in the group-based intervention and these new and modified sessions were continually enhanced as the program reached a larger range of young GBQ men. There were three primary factors that were identified by the participants as forces that increased their likelihood of engaging in unsafe sexual behavior, including: (a) substance use, (b) depression, and (c) sexual objectification by older White men. The issue of substance use was incorporated into a new session that explored some of the reasons why GBQ young men use substances (e.g., pleasure, escape, "fitting in"), and the decreased rates of condom use associated with using substances prior to sex. Depression was also addressed in a new session that included a more general focus on the psychological stressors associated with being GBQ in an oppressive society, and the ways in which this can lead to feelings of depression and loneliness. The link between depression and increased risk of participation in unsafe sex also was explored.

Sexual objectification by older White men was addressed in several of the sessions. The power differential that exists between younger GBQ men of color and older more experienced White gay/bisexual men in romantic and sexual relationships was explored with participants in a session devoted to dating and relationships. This was also addressed in the session on self-esteem since feelings of self-doubt and insecurity experienced by several of the participants lead them to be vulnerable to coercive acts by older White men who would persuade them to have unprotected sex, as well as in the general session on HIV sexual risk and protective behaviors.

In addition to these specific content areas, the youth expressed general concerns regarding "coming out" to friends and family members, anxiety about feeling comfortable in the larger gay community, and fears about verbal/physical harassment. A new session was added on "Coming Out" that included group discussion and interactive activities, as well as an additional session on "Navigating the Gay Community" which helped participants to better understand the diversity of the larger "gay community," and to explore their personal place in that community. The issue of harassment was addressed by adding a session on personal safety that included a discussion with a representative from a community organization focused on LGBT human rights.

BENEFITS OF THE COLLABORATIVE PROCESS EVALUATION

There have been multiple benefits to all parties involved in this process evaluation. Because of their participation, Project VIDA has become more structured in various aspects of how the agency operates and thus has developed more efficient and effective ways to document prevention efforts. The agency has terminated the use of awkward forms that were previously completed but not used. Prior to the collaboration, many of the procedures were passed on by word of mouth, and most documentation was unstructured and inconsistent. Participation in the partnership also resulted in efforts to better define the roles and responsibilities of staff members involved in the programs, and helped to offer accountability for their time. As a result of new agency and program meetings and procedures, there also has been an increase in staff communication. Overall, participation in the collaborative project increased the capacity of Project VIDA to design, implement and evaluate their prevention efforts, as well as their capacity to obtain funding for their prevention initiatives. Following participation in this project, Project VIDA increased their portfolio of prevention programs from the two described in this article to six fully funded HIV prevention programs.

Agency staff members who were involved in the collaborative team also benefited from their participation in the evaluation project. They improved their group facilitation skills by receiving direct feedback after sessions by non-participant observers, attending trainings, and making more effective use of clinical supervision by maintaining their group facilitator journal. They also gained extensive knowledge about various aspects of scientifically sound, comprehensive program evaluation, and have been increasing their contact and networking with others in the local HIV prevention field through participation in both academic and service-oriented meetings. In addition, the staff have made contact with other agencies outside of Chicago who work with similar populations in order to improve their prevention programs.

Youth from the community also have benefited greatly. Participants in both prevention programs have learned how to protect themselves from infection with HIV in programs that are culturally and developmentally appropriate. In addition, since the programs address the specific environmental and social stressors that the participants face in their community, the youth are able to develop the coping skills and protective self-efficacy needed to further reduce their risk. Youth who have participated in the intervention have also been given the opportunity to interact with other young people who are experiencing similar life experiences and who share similar cultural and life histories. Thus, many have developed friendships with other participants and have created new social support networks that serve to reinforce health-promoting practices.

Finally, many of the youth that have participated in the focus groups and interviews have expressed their excitement about being able to actually play a part in the shaping of the prevention programs. Some of these youth have become volunteers for the two programs after they participated in the group-based sessions. Thus, they have been able to have additional input into the modification of the programs and have witnessed the ways in which their suggestions have been implemented. The youth often talk about their concerns with the array of negative influences in their communities, and their desire to help others that may be at risk for negative health outcomes such as HIV infection. By participating in the process evaluation, they have felt empowered, since the information they offered is used to improve the programs for future youth.

CONCLUSIONS

The collaborative process evaluation described in this article was largely successful because of the collaborative team's empowerment evaluation focus and use of a narrative ethnographic approach that explored the multiple elements of environment and culture that impact the sexual health of Latina female adolescents and GBQ Latino and African-American male adolescents. The information gathered and analyzed during the process evaluation was used to revise Project VIDA's HIV prevention efforts so that they more accurately addressed the specific social, cultural, and environmental factors that impact youths' participation in HIV risk behaviors, and also helped young people in the community to create new empowering narratives.

Future collaborations between evaluators and CBOs should be developed to conduct process evaluations aimed at improving prevention programs for oppressed and marginalized communities. In order to increase both the amount of funding for process evaluations and the frequency with which community agencies conduct process evaluations, knowledge about the types, benefits, and methods of process evaluation must be shared on a variety of levels (e.g., between program evaluators, funding agencies, CBOs, and agency staff members). Program evaluators should encourage CBOs to conduct process evaluations prior to outcome evaluations, or in lieu of outcome evaluations when appropriate. Funders also need to be cognizant of the benefits of process evaluation, especially with regard to the ways in which such evaluations can help CBOs improve and standardize their programs prior to conducting outcome evaluations.

REFERENCES

Catania, J. A., Kegeles, S. M., & Coates, T. J. (1990). Towards an understanding of risk behavior: An AIDS risk reduction model (ARRM). *Health Education Quarterly, 17*, 53-72.

Diaz, R. M. (1998). *Latino gay men and HIV.* New York: Routledge.

Fetterman, D. M. (1996). Empowerment evaluation: An introduction to theory and practice. In D. M. Fetterman, S. J. Kaftarian, & A. Wandersman (Eds.). *Empowerment evaluation: Knowledge and tools for self-assessment and accountability.* Thousand Oaks, CA: Sage.

Gottfredson, D. C., Fink, C. M., Skroban, S., & Gottfredson, G. D. (1997). Making prevention work. In R. P. Weissberg & T. P. Gullotta (Eds.), *Healthy children 2010: Establishing preventive services. Issues in children's and families' lives,* Vol. 9. Thousand Oaks, CA: Sage.

Harper, G. W., Bangi, A. K., Contreras, R., Pedraza, A., Tolliver, M., & Vess, L. (in press). Diverse phases of collaboration: Working together to improve community-based HIV interventions for youth. *American Journal of Community Psychology.*

Harper, G. W., Lardon, C., Rappaport, J., Bangi, A. K., Contreras, R., & Pedraza, A. (2004). Community narratives: The use of narrative ethnography in participatory community research. In L. Jason, C. Keys, Y. Suarez-Balcazar, R. R. Taylor, M. Davis, J. Durlak, & D. Isenberg (Eds), *Participatory Community Research: Theories and Methods in Action.* Washington, DC: American Psychological Association.

Harper, G. W., & Salina, D. (2000). Building collaborative partnerships to improve community-based HIV prevention research: The university-CBO collaborative partnership (UCCP) model. *Journal of Prevention & Intervention in the Community, 19,* 1-20.

Holland, J., Ramazanoglu, C., Sharpe, S., & Thomson, R. (1994). Achieving masculine sexuality: Young men's strategies for managing vulnerability. In L. Doyal, J. Naidoo, & T. Wilton (Eds.), *AIDS: Setting a feminist agenda* (pp. 122-148). London: Taylor & Francis.

Linney, J. A. & Wandersman, A. (1991). *Prevention plus III: Assessing alcohol and other drug prevention programs at the school and community level: A four-step guide to useful program assessment.* Washington, DC: US Department of Health & Human Services.

Mankowski, E. S., & Rappaport, J. (2000). Narrative concepts and analysis in spiritually based communities. *Journal of Community Psychology, 28*(5), 479-493.

Miller, R. L., & Cassel, J. B. (2000). Ongoing evaluation in AIDS-service organizations: Building meaningful evaluation activities. *Journal of Prevention & Intervention in the Community, 19*(1), 21-40.

Nelson, G., Prilleltensky, I., & MacGillivary, H. (2001). Building value-based partnerships: Toward solidarity with oppressed groups. *American Journal of Community Psychology, 29,* 649-677.

Rappaport, J. (1998). The art of social change: Community narratives as resources for individual and collective identity. In X. B. Arriaga & S. Oskamp (Eds.), *Addressing community problems: Psychosocial research and intervention* (pp. 225-246). Thousand Oaks, CA: Sage.

Rappaport, J. (2000). Community narratives: Tales of terror and joy. *American Journal of Community Psychology, 28*(2), 1-24.

Zimmerman, M. A. (2000). Empowerment theory: Psychological, organizational, and community levels of analysis. In J. Rappaport & E. Seidman (Eds.), *Handbook of community psychology.* New York: Plenum.

Collaborative Program Development and Evaluation: A Case Study in Conflict Resolution Education

Carolyn G. Benne

Georgia State University

Wendy M. Garrard

Vanderbilt University

SUMMARY. This is a story of collaboration between program developers and an evaluator to support the design of the Conflict Resolution in Schools Programs (CRiSP) community initiative. We discuss a variety of evaluation techniques useful in program development to illustrate the

Address correspondence to: Carolyn Benne, Consortium on Negotiation and Conflict Resolution, College of Law, Georgia State University, P.O. Box 4037, Atlanta, GA 30302-4037 (E-mail: *cbenne@gsu.edu*). Meta-analysis details can be obtained from Wendy Garrard, Center for Evaluation Research and Methodology, Vanderbilt Institute for Public Policy Studies, 1207 18th Avenue South, Nashville, TN 37212 (E-mail: *wendy.garrard@vanderbilt.edu*).

This research was supported in part by grants from the U.S. Department of Education, in conjunction with the Albany Law School, by the Fund for the Improvement of Post-Secondary Education (FIPSE) Grant 84.116A [Application P116B80419]; and the National Institute of Mental Health Grant RO1-MH57766.

[Haworth co-indexing entry note]: "Collaborative Program Development and Evaluation: A Case Study in Conflict Resolution Education." Benne, Carolyn G., and Wendy M. Garrard. Co-published simultaneously in *Journal of Prevention & Intervention in the Community* (The Haworth Press, Inc.) Vol. 26, No. 2, 2003, pp. 71-87; and: *Empowerment and Participatory Evaluation of Community Interventions: Multiple Benefits* (ed: Yolanda Suarez-Balcazar, and Gary W. Harper) The Haworth Press, Inc., 2003, pp. 71-87. Single or multiple copies of this article are available for a fee from The Haworth Document Delivery Service [1-800-HAWORTH, 9:00 a.m. - 5:00 p.m. (EST). E-mail address: docdelivery@haworthpress.com].

10.1300/J005v26n02_06

benefits of a collaborative approach. The formative stages of the initiative included needs assessment and traditional literature review, followed by the design, implementation, and monitoring of pilot programs. Based on the questions that emerged in the formative research, we launched a comprehensive meta-analysis of conflict resolution education programs to guide the future efforts of the CRiSP initiative. We describe the stages of CRiSP research to date and present highlights of the results from the first two years of formative work and evaluability assessment. Preliminary results of the meta-analysis that describe the predominant characteristics of thirty conflict management programs in primary and secondary schools are also included. *[Article copies available for a fee from The Haworth Document Delivery Service: 1-800-HAWORTH. E-mail address: <docdelivery@haworthpress.com> Website: <http://www. HaworthPress.com> © 2003 by The Haworth Press, Inc. All rights reserved.]*

KEYWORDS. Collaboration, conflict resolution in schools, meta-analysis

Evaluation scholars and researchers have long advocated that procedures for monitoring and assessing program performance should be embedded during the early stages of program planning and implementation (Bickman, 1994; Chelimsky, 1994; Rossi, Freeman, & Lipsey, 1999). Doing so greatly increases the options for rigorous evaluation designs, stakeholder participation, and ongoing program improvement. Unfortunately, most program evaluations are planned long after a program has been established. Consequently, there are few examples available as to how program development and evaluation may be integrated in practice. This case study of a school-based conflict resolution education (CRE) program provides such an example, emphasizing the benefits realized by both program developers and evaluator when they collaborate to launch a new program.

The Conflict Resolution in Schools Program (CRiSP) research initiative illustrates the benefits of integrating evaluation concepts, techniques, and findings as part of the design and implementation of a community-based program. The evaluative perspective allowed the program developer to avoid pitfalls, conserve resources, learn valuable lessons, and ultimately produce results which were well-suited to guide subsequent efforts. To establish the context for the collaborative process between the evaluator and the program developer, we first describe the overall CRiSP initiative. Next, we present the collaborative research methods used and highlights from the project's findings. We conclude with lessons learned from our collaboration that strengthened the research process and enhanced our ability to work together.

CONFLICT RESOLUTION IN SCHOOLS PROGRAM: A CASE STUDY

In 1998, CNCR obtained funding for the Conflict Resolution in Schools Program to develop a framework to guide the design, implementation, institutionalization, and evaluation of conflict resolution education (CRE) programs in schools serving children from kindergarten through grade 12.

While evaluation methods are commonly reserved for use after a program is established, evaluation strategies–particularly evaluability assessment–are remarkably helpful tools for program development (Bickman, 1994; Chelimsky, 1994; Patton, 1997; Rossi, Freeman, & Lipsey, 1999; Smith, 1989; Wholey, 1987). Taking advantage of this approach, the CRiSP program developers required that evaluative research be embedded throughout all phases of the CRiSP initiative and invited an evaluator to collaborate prior to project start-up.

The three-year multi-method project entailed a complex agenda. A multidisciplinary CRiSP team of program developers (CNCR administrators, conflict resolution professionals, and post-secondary practicum students) and an external evaluator was assembled to develop, implement, and evaluate CRE programming. To enhance the integration of program development and evaluation throughout each stage of the project, the program development team established three guiding principles: (a) the research process would be collaborative and aimed at building CRiSP's internal capacity for evaluation, (b) the keystones of the CRiSP framework would be developed by identifying specific needs in the school settings and by applying the program logic model, and (c) the roles of program developers and evaluator would be clarified and redefined as they evolved throughout the process (for a full discussion of social science research roles see Druckman [2000]). These principles reflect our commitment to the challenging task of balancing the traditional evaluation goals of program improvement and accountability with the stakeholder's need for self-determination and capacity-building (Fawcett, Paine-Andrews, Francisco, Schultz, Richter et al., 1996).

Conflict resolution education programs expose youth to conflict resolution knowledge, skills, and techniques to help them constructively resolve interpersonal disputes. These programs have become one of the most popular means of addressing behavioral and social problems in public schools. Conservative estimates show an increase from 2,000 to over 8,500 programs nationwide during the last decade (Jones & Kmitta, 2000; National Association for Mediation in Education, 1994). Unfortunately, there is little rigorous evidence available to confirm or dispute the effectiveness of CRE in school settings (for a review see Deutsch & Coleman, 2000; Johnson & Johnson, 1996; Jones & Kmitta, 2000; Webster, 1993).

To address the paucity of research in this area, CRiSP aims to systematically consolidate existing CRE program theory and evidence. This ambitious project involved (a) conducting needs assessments, (b) reviewing the existing literature, (c) examining primary data from pilot programs, (d) synthesizing secondary data from outside programs using meta-analysis, and (e) working with other leaders in the field to propose comprehensive guidelines for designing and evaluating school-based CRE programs tailored for individual settings. The following section provides an overview of the CRiSP initiative's participants and activities. Relevant highlights from the collaborative experience of the program developers and evaluator are presented to illustrate the roles assumed by each in CRE program design.

PROJECT OVERVIEW

The CRiSP team identified multiple stakeholder groups and employed a variety of research methods to gather information about typical conflicts and procedures for conflict resolution in Pre-K through grade 12 schools. The team was directed by two CNCR conflict management professionals and included 26 university students (19 females and 7 males ranging from 19 to 54 years of age; 57% were African-American, 41% Anglo-American, and 2% Hispanic) that participated as part of a two-semester elective service-learning practicum, 6 project mentors from the local Bar Association, and an external evaluator.

The sites selected for the CRiSP pilot programs were part of a single school cluster (a high school with multiple lower grade feeder schools) in a metropolitan area in the Southeast. The three public schools (an elementary, middle, and high school) represented a diverse range of participants including students, school administrators, counselors, teachers, parents, and affiliated personnel such as police officers and staff of other programs operating in the school setting, and community groups outside the schools involved in support activities such as mentoring.

This project involved both primary and secondary data and empha-sized a mixed methods approach. Primary data collection included structured interviews, focus groups and paper-and-pencil surveys at all three schools with a broad sample from the key stakeholder groups. As-sessment questions focused on the types and circumstances of conflict in each school, and the existing procedures and resources for managing the conflicts. Behavior checklists and field journals were also used to document conflict behaviors in classrooms and public areas throughout the program timeframe. Secondary data sources included school poli-cies and procedures, discipline referral records and results from other CRE programs.

PHASES OF CRiSP DEVELOPMENT

Program development occurred in three overlapping phases and fol-lowed established principles of conflict management system design (see Costantino and Merchant, 1996; Ury, Brett and Goldberg, 1988). The phases included: initial planning and evaluation of needs in pilot sites; design, implementation, and evaluability assessment of pilot pro-grams; and comprehensive follow-up research and development.

Phase I: Initial Planning and Identification of Needs

Phase I included two main components: (a) articulation of program logic, and (b) identification of needs in the target schools that could real-istically be addressed by the program. The CRiSP team used *evaluability assessment* as a systematic way to assess a program's ability to function as planned and fulfill its goals. Evaluability assessment strategies most useful in program development include: articulating program logic and goals, identifying activities and resources needed to accomplish these goals, determining potential sources of primary and secondary data, and providing rapid feedback to the program stakeholders (for a full discussion of evaluability see Smith, 1989; and Wholey, 1987). By combining their knowledge and skills, the CRiSP program developers and evaluator were able to construct a model of the CRE logic, and to encourage ob-jectivity in determining whether the intended program was a realistic fit in each school.

Articulation of program logic. A good program logic model clearly defines the set of means-end assumptions about how a program pro-duces changes in human behaviors, cognitions, or circumstances to meet its intended goals, thus increasing the likelihood that program resources will be used effectively to target the intended outcomes (for a full discussion of program logic see Rossi, Freeman, & Lipsey, 1999; and Smith, 1989). The logic model for CRE curriculum emerged from a step-wise process developed by the authors (Benne & Garrard, 2000). The evaluator facilitated four group discussions with program developers from July to September 1999. Between meetings, a Delphi-type consensus process was used to circulate evolving versions of the logic model among the developers to clarify and refine the collective ideas. After circulating several versions, the CRiSP team achieved consensus on a working logic model which broadly defined the content areas for CRE curriculum.

The logic model represented major progress toward clarification of important programmatic issues such as the overall goals and boundaries of the CRiSP initiative, curriculum content, the target population, and molar strategies for curriculum delivery based on accepted theory and practice from the CRE literature. The foundational elements of the CRE curriculum were designed to enhance the participants' ability of to *exercise self-control* when faced with an interpersonal conflict, to *use effective communication* skills to *analyze conflict situations* (e.g., social perspective-taking and related cognitions about self and others), to *engage in problem solving strategies*, and to *follow through with options for resolution.*

Evaluation of needs in the school settings. Program procedures and goals are not always compatible with the structure of the target setting (e.g., priorities, facilities, time constraints, and administration policy), even when based on strong logic and a thorough literature review. In addition, the nature and functions of interpersonal conflict vary greatly depending on the people and settings involved. Therefore, before attempting to design or implement any CRE program, a needs assessment should be conducted to determine if the needs of the target site may be effectively addressed by CRE.

The CRiSP team was responsible for collecting needs assessment data. This role allowed the team members to build rapport with the stakeholders in the future program sites. The evaluator supported the CRiSP team members by assisting with the design and use of needs assessment methods, and by challenging them to consider the fit between the goals and capacities of their program and the needs of the target environment.

From August 1999 to January 2000, the CRiSP team gathered and summarized data from a wide range of stakeholders in each of the target schools. The effort yielded a wealth of information about the nature of conflict in each school setting, uncovered a diverse range of existing mechanisms and resources for managing conflict in each setting, and identified several options for working with school stakeholders.

The major concern arising from the needs assessment data was that school administrators held unrealistic expectations about the scope and severity of the student behaviors that CRiSP would address. The program developers had to revisit the issue of target population with school administrators, and ultimately it was agreed that CRiSP would not be designed to assist children with serious and chronic emotional or behavioral issues. After clarifying the program's purpose, the developers decided to proceed with design and implementation of pilot programs in the target sites.

Phase II: Design and Implementation in Target Schools

In Phase II, the CRiSP team designed and implemented three very different CRE programs in the target elementary, middle and high schools. The individualized designs were based on the needs assessment findings from Phase I.

Elementary school site. The pilot program in the elementary site offered two opportunities for exposure to the CRE curriculum: classroom instruction and an after-school program. University practicum students used commercial curricula modules (e.g., Bodine & Crawford, 1998) to provide 30 minutes of classroom instruction two times per week in two separate third-grade classrooms from January through May 2000. Approximately 75 participants received this instruction. University practicum students also conducted two hours of after-school programming two to three days each week for three semesters beginning in January 2000. Approximately 12 participants from kindergarten through fifth grade attended the after-school program on any given day. In a typical program session, the university practicum students employed experiential strategies such as role-play and cooperative learning activities to engage participants in a selected CRE topic.

Middle school site. A second group of university practicum students piloted CRE curriculum as an elective class for sixth- and seventh grade participants from January 2000 through May 2001. Participants who received the training included some who opted to enroll as well as some recommended by the school administrators. The curriculum consisted of commercially available modules and was administered in five 40-minute classes per week for a class cycle of nine weeks. A total of six class cycles was offered, with approximately 12 participants enrolled in each cycle. At least two university practicum students were present for each class, and they were regularly monitored by a CRiSP project director and assisted by CRiSP mentors from the community Bar Association. Established curriculum modules were selected to match each element of the CRE logic model (e.g., Kriedler, 1994), and a variety of teaching strategies were used to engage the participants including role play, games, group discussions, and keeping a journal.

High school site. A third group of university practicum students offered CRE curriculum as an elective course for 10th-grade participants during regular school hours beginning in January 2000. Although 20 participants opted to enroll in the course, a maximum of 6 participants attended on any given day from January through March 2000. The CRiSP team worked closely with school administrators to restructure the course to ensure more consistent attendance. However, they were unable to find a suitable solution, and the course was cancelled by mid-semester.

Evaluability Issues for Elementary and Middle School Pilots

Review of pilot data showed that, in spite of program limitations, the overall perceptions of the program developers and the school stakeholders were positive. The school personnel reported that the programs had provided much-needed resources and assistance for addressing problem student behaviors, and the CRE participants reported the learning experiences were beneficial. The university practicum students demonstrated a strong commitment to their service-learning responsibilities throughout the pilot programs, and the majority reported it had been a highly beneficial experience.

Several areas of concern were identified in the evaluability assessment of the pilot programs. The immediate concerns for the design of future programs included the sufficiency of the program components, adequacy of program resources, and the availability of criteria and standards for assessing program performance.

Sufficiency of program components. The program components were implemented with reasonable fidelity to the intended design, and were viewed positively by school stakeholders and the university practicum students. A notable exception was the commercial curricula used. The university practicum students found the commercial materials failed to engage participants. Feedback from the CRE participants revealed the materials were outdated, contained unrealistic content, and immature subject matter. The most effective program materials were modifications of the commercial curricula that capitalized on the real-life experiences of the elementary and middle school participants.

Adequacy of program resources. The level of implementation in elementary and middle school sites was ambitious, and it proved difficult to sustain with the resources allocated. Although there were several university practicum students assigned to each pilot site, their academic schedules limited participation at times. For example, they were not consistently available when the school provided access to community stakeholders for the needs assessment. In addition, when the university practicum students staffed the CRE activities on a rotating basis, the lack of a consistent presence in the classroom each day appeared to contribute to classroom management issues and disruptive participant behavior. The short-term solution was to have a CRiSP administrator present each day. Unfortunately, this intensive support could not be sustained indefinitely.

Criteria and standards for program performance. The pilot research considered a number of indicators of participant engagement and learning. We found that the measures available for assessing interpersonal conflict and resolution are of limited use for purposes of assessing the effectiveness of CRE programs. The most widely recommended measures proved either too labor intensive (e.g., in-depth observations), invasive (e.g., the community school board found videotaped performance problematic), confounded with other issues (e.g., discipline records do not distinguish between constructive and destructive conflict behaviors), or not suitable for this population (e.g., ceiling effects) or program curriculum (e.g., not specific to the CRE components). For example, the pre-post surveys used to assess the learning gains in the middle school demonstrated ceiling effects and were not congruent with the behavioral observations (attributed to social desirability bias).

Finally, it was difficult for the university practicum students and the school stakeholders to adhere to the CRiSP goals and program boundaries as designed. For example, teachers persistently referred elementary and middle school participants with serious behavior or emotional problems to the program. This had a negative result on the program over time, as CRE participants began to view the class as targeting remedial behavior and "problem students." This referral pattern was not congruent with the program's intention to provide CRE as prevention rather than intervention. The influx of these children also caused problems for the university practicum students. Many of the CRiSP team members were discouraged at their inadequacy to address participant needs that were more appropriate for professional mediators, counselors, or social workers (e.g., parent-school conflict, and psychological support for seriously disturbed or abused children).

Overall, the knowledge gained during the pilot programs provided valuable first-hand information about the challenges, strengths, and limitations of designing and implementing CRE programs in school settings. The information gathered in Phases I and II was reviewed, and the findings were used to shape the agenda for the next phase of intensive research and development.

Phase III: Comprehensive Research and Development

Phase III moves closer to the CRiSP initiative's primary goal by synthesizing research from a number of sources. The information will be used to develop a practical framework for guiding the design, implementation, and evaluation of sustainable CRE programs in school settings. The framework will be driven by evidence of what constitutes best practices in CRE to date. Phase III involves two consecutive components: (a) a meta-analysis of the treatment effectiveness research to date from the CRE literature, followed by (b) review and interpretation of evidence by a panel of experts from a diverse range of school-based CRE research and practice. The meta-analysis is part of the larger body of information reviewed by the panel of experts beginning in October, 2002. We share preliminary highlights from the meta-analysis below, and you may contact the first author for more information about the CRE expert panel review.

The two broad objectives for the meta-analysis were (a) to describe the predominant characteristics of CRE programs and (b) to determine whether the effects of these programs varied by age or by the CRE curriculum components proposed in the CRiSP model in Phase I. From a collaborative perspective, the program developers and evaluator switched roles during this phase, as the evaluator's technical skills necessarily took precedence throughout the meta-analysis. However, the program developer's specialized knowledge of conflict theory and practice informed the meta-analysis design, which was grounded in the CRE logic model components from Phase I.

The studies in this meta-analysis were drawn from an ongoing comprehensive database established specifically for meta-analytic research on intervention programs for risk factors of antisocial behaviors among youth (Lipsey, 1997).[1] Studies from the *Early Intervention* meta-analysis database were included in the present analysis if they met both of the following additional criteria: (a) the dominant intervention protocol explicitly involved interpersonal conflict resolution in a school setting, and (b) compared a control group with a treatment group. The meta-analysis was conducted using standardized mean effect sizes as recommended in Lipsey and Wilson (2001).

Thirty CRE studies were eligible for this analysis. The eligible studies were all reported after 1979, with most (76%) reported between 1995 and 2001. Two-thirds of the studies were dissertations; one-third was journal articles, and one study was a conference paper. All studies were conducted for research purposes, and the programs had been established less than two years prior to the data collection and reporting.

Preliminary Results of the CRE Meta-Analysis

Sample characteristics. The studies represent a total of 4,225 school-age participants with a median sample size of 78 (two-thirds of the sample sizes ranged between 42 and 126; full range = 16 to 1,414) across all studies. The studies included the full range of school-age youth, with 16% of the samples from elementary grades, 48% from middle school grades, and 36% from high schools. The race and ethnicity of the samples were reported in two-thirds of the samples, with 44% Anglo-American and 16% African-American. For the remaining third, no specific race or ethnicity information was reported.

Program characteristics. Ninety-three percent of the programs explicitly provided training in mainstream conflict resolution concepts and skills, such as mediation and negotiation. Among the components identified in the CRiSP model of conflict education (see Phase I), the most prevalent specialized characteristics of the conflict management interventions were communication training (76%), situation analysis (66%), and social problem solving (62%). The least represented CRE curriculum component was self-control (24%). The typical conflict management treatment was administered for less than 2 hours per week for 7 weeks, with 52% of the studies averaging between 10 to 20 hours of total exposure. The most prevalent format among teaching strategies was role-play or rehearsal (62%), followed by provision of non-interactive information such as lecture (45%) and interactive group discussion (35%).

Main effects. A mean aggregate effect size (*ES*) of .39 (*SD* = .35; *95% CI* = .22 to .55; *Q* = 125.26, *df* = 29, *p* = .000) was found across all 30 studies. The mean *ES* value indicates that, across all 30 studies, the participant groups receiving CRE performed an average of .39 standard deviations better than the comparison groups. The significant *Q*-value shows the variability among the studies is higher than would be expected due to sampling error, and further examination of subgroup differences is warranted. A full exploration of the potential sources of variance is beyond the scope of this paper.[2] For current exploratory purposes, the primary question was whether the effects of CRE programs vary by age. Using a meta-analysis analog for analysis of variance, main effects were obtained for age, with significant mean effects for middle grades ($ES = .40, N = 14$, 95% $CI = .17$ to $.63$; $Q_{df = 13} = 10.65, p = .47$), and for high school grades ($ES = .40, N = 11$, 95% $CI = .08$ to $.72$; $Q_{df = 10} = 6.97, p = .54$). No significant effect was detected for the small subset of studies in elementary grades ($ES = .32, N = 5$, 95% $CI = -.08$ to $.72$; $Q_{df = 4} = 3.34, p = .34$). (See Table 1).

Conditional effects. The analysis plan called for the breakout of mean effects for each of the CRiSP logic model components discussed in Phase I. However, the gaps in the CRE outcome literature do not currently provide sufficient empirical data to address this issue. In spite of the relatively widespread inclusion of these components in CRE curricula, among the 30 CRE studies examined here, few reported outcomes for these distinct components (communication = 1, situation analysis = 5, social problem-solving = 3, and self-control = 3).

TABLE 1. Standardized Mean Effects for Conflict Resolution Education with School-Age Youth

Source	N	ES[a]	SE	95% CI Lower	95% CI Upper	df	Q[b]
Overall mean effect across all studies	30	.39**	.08	.22	.55	29	125.26**
Effects for school-age groups[c]							
Between						2	.11
Within						27	20.98
Total						29	21.09
Pre-K and elementary grades	5	.32	.21	−.08	.72	4	3.34
Middle school	14	.40**	.12	.17	.63	13	10.65
High school	11	.40*	.16	.08	.72	10	6.97

[a]Standardized mean difference effect size for treatment vs. control groups; positive values indicate the treatment group obtained a more desirable score relative to the control group.
[b]Q-test for homogeneity of sample of studies.
[c]Based on a mixed effects model using the MetaF computation developed by Lipsey and Wilson (2001).
*$p < .05$. **$p < .01$.

DISCUSSION

This is the story of a successful collaboration that resulted in well-defined objectives and clear implementation plans, yielded a wealth of qualitative real-world data, and subsequently led to a quantitative meta-analytic review in search of answers to practical questions about CRE program design. The information gathered over the course of this project to date suggests that conflict resolution education does have potential applications in school settings that warrant further research. However, we also discovered a number of obstacles to the design, administration and monitoring of programs that meet the real-world needs of schools to help students resolve interpersonal conflicts.

The area of greatest concern for program design is the appropriateness of commercial programs to address the specific issues of individual schools. The CRE field needs evidence-based information about which curriculum components should be included, and how they may be delivered most effectively to different age groups. The preliminary meta-analytic work has revealed important gaps in the literature that need to be addressed by primary research. For example, it is problematic that 23 out of 30 CRE programs included some form of communication training as part of the intervention, but only one program included a measure of communication in the assessment battery. The field of CRE must do a better job of examining the effectiveness of the various curriculum components, including social problem-solving, perspective-taking, and self-regulation of social affect; and of understanding the mechanisms that connect them.

The most pressing question to emerge from the CRiSP fieldwork involves how to determine when CRE is well matched to the conflict needs of a school. Even though the CRiSP teams custom-tailored programs to address selected needs in the target sites, the needs appropriately met by CRE were not the highest priority from the school's perspective. Time after time, the schools' needs tested the boundaries of the CRiSP initiative by requesting assistance with behavior problems which were not appropriately addressed by CRE. As a result, this research initiative encourages other CRE programs to join in the task of clarifying the boundaries of CRE so that schools may make informed decisions as to when CRE programs will meet their specific needs.

LESSONS LEARNED FROM THE CRiSP COLLABORATION

The collaborative approach undertaken in this project led to valuable lessons that will inform the future work of the CRiSP initiative and should be useful to other collaborative efforts as well. The atypical ingredient in this case study was the program developers' strong commitment to using evaluative research in all phases of their project. They relied on the evaluation perspective to clarify goals, assess the needs of the target sites, monitor progress in relation to program goals, and use feedback from the monitoring to stimulate continuous program improvement.

From the program developer's perspective, the participatory approach to evaluation provided clarity of purpose that made program design efficient and rewarding, as well as building their capacity for conducting evaluation. The strongest illustration of increased clarity in program design was the articulation of the program logic model. Prior to developing the logic model, CNCR personnel assumed they agreed about the program goals and procedures. For example, some members expected CRiSP to be a demonstration project, which could be used as an example for other CRE programs. Others expected it to reduce the overall destructive conflict related to crime and delinquency in the community. The team eventually achieved genuine consensus about important programming issues, which served them well in later phases of this complex project.

The value of having true group consensus on program logic was most evident when conflict arose between the expressed needs of the schools and the program objectives in the pilot sites. For example, when the schools referred participants who were not appropriate for the CRiSP objectives, the program developers were able to keep the program reasonably on track by vigilant monitoring of the program implementation and participants. They credited their effective monitoring system to the group's commitment to the objectives identified through the construction of the logic model.

From the evaluator's perspective, this collaboration provided an opportunity to learn strategies for participatory processes from the conflict management professionals at CNCR. The program logic model also provides an example of how the evaluator benefited from cross-discipline learning. A pivotal concept in group facilitation is that the facilitator guides the process, not the content. The facilitator is present as a neutral third party to help stakeholders express and accomplish their goals. Having the evaluator assume the role of facilitator is consistent with the values of participatory evaluation as well as with most approaches to articulating program logic (see Suarez-Balcazar & Orellana-Damacela, 1999). The added value from the conflict management perspective is an emphasis on defining the participant roles and purposes of group participation. For example, by clarifying the roles each partner would assume, the evaluator was better able to serve as a neutral facilitator in the logic model discussions, encouraging the program developers to debate the ideas fully. When the roles are not clearly understood in advance, the involvement of the evaluator may unintentionally suppress the debate process. By functioning as an active, but skillfully neutral, member of the program logic discussions, the evaluator could draw attention more constructively to any discrepancies in the program developers' perceptions of the goals and objectives. We believe this approach helped the CRiSP team to balance the dual goals of program improvement and self-determination (Fawcett, Paine-Andrews, Francisco, Schultz, Richter et al., 1996).

The final lesson emphasized here is perhaps the most important–to engage in active learning about collaboration. Our experience suggests that collaboration in real-world research is most successful when the program developers and evaluators (or researchers) explicitly discuss and orchestrate their roles. Program developers and evaluators have distinct responsibilities in a research initiative, even when they work closely as partners. When their working relationship is structured around the specific needs and objectives of a project, program developers and evaluators are better able to create a bridge between two important types of knowledge: *evidence*, gained through rigorous research; and *wisdom*, derived from innovative practice in the field (Slaby, 1998). Throughout the CRiSP initiative the process of articulating our roles increased our awareness of the potential contributions of the individual team members, made us more open to new ideas, and expanded our knowledge beyond the traditional boundaries of our respective disciplines. We encourage others to explore new ways for practitioner-evaluator collaborations to be defined and implemented.

NOTES

1. The Early Intervention database is composed of studies involving psychological, educational, or behavioral interventions for non-delinquent youth less than 18 years of age. To date it includes 576 studies reporting on 1,273 treatment and comparison groups. All studies were reported in English between 1950 and June 2001, and yielded at least one quantitative effect size for a risk factor empirically associated with antisocial behavior (Lipsey & Derzon, 1998).

2. A comprehensive meta-analysis of school-based CRE programs is underway and additional information may be obtained from the second author.

REFERENCES

Benne, C. G., & Garrard, W. M. (2000). *Logic model as method: The nuts and bolts of logic model construction.* Paper presented at the annual meeting of the American Evaluation Association, Honolulu, HI.

Bickman, L. (1994). An optimistic view of evaluation. *Evaluation Practice, 15,* 255-259.

Bodine, R., & Crawford, D. (1998). *The handbook of conflict resolution education: A guide to building quality programs in schools.* San Francisco: Jossey-Bass.

Chelimsky, E. (1994). Evaluation: Where we are. *Evaluation Practice, 15,* 339-345.

Costantino, C., & Merchant, C. (1996). *Designing conflict management systems: A guide to creating productive and healthy organizations.* San Francisco: Jossey-Bass.

Deutsch, M., & Coleman, P. T. (Eds.). (2000). *The handbook of conflict resolution: Theory and practice.* San Francisco: Jossey-Bass.

Druckman, D. (2000). Frameworks, techniques, and theory: Contributions of research consulting in social science. *American Behavioral Scientist, 43,* 1635-1666.

Fawcett, S. B., Paine-Andrews, A., Francisco, V. T., Schultz, J. A., Richter, K. P., Lewis, R. K., Harris, K. J., Williams, E. L., Berkley, J. Y., Lopez, C. M., & Fisher, J. L. (1996). Empowering community health initiatives through evaluation. In D. M. Fetterman, S. J. Kaftarian, & A. Wandersman (Eds.), *Empowerment evaluation: Knowledge and tools for self-assessment and accountability* (pp. 161-187). Thousand Oaks, CA: Sage.

Johnson, D.W., & Johnson, R. (1996). Conflict resolution and peer mediation programs in elementary and secondary schools: A review of the research. *Review of Educational Research, 66,* 459-506.

Jones, T. S., & Kmitta, D. (Eds.). (2000). *Does it work? The case for conflict resolution education in our nation's schools.* Washington, DC: Conflict Resolution Education Network.

Kriedler, W. J. (1994). *Conflict resolution in the middle school: A curriculum and teacher's guide.* Cambridge, MA: Educators for Social Responsibility. *Early intervention database on risk for antisocial behavior in children and youth: 1997-2002* [Data file]. Nashville, TN: Center for Evaluation Research and Methodology, Vanderbilt University.

Lipsey, M. W., & Wilson, D. B. (2001). *Practical meta-analysis.* Thousand Oaks, CA: Sage.

National Association for Mediation in Education. (1994). *Conflict resolution: Solving conflicts without violence.* Amherst, MA: Author.

Patton, M. Q. (1997). *Utilization-focused evaluation: The new century text.* Thousand Oaks, CA: Sage.

Rossi, P. H., Freeman, H. E., & Lipsey, M. W. (1999). *Evaluation: A systematic approach.* Thousand Oaks, CA: Sage.

Slaby, R. G. (1998). Preventing violence through research-guided intervention. In P. K. Trickett & C. J. Schellenback (Eds.), *Violence against children in the family and the community* (pp. 371-399). Washington, DC: American Psychological Association.

Smith, M. F. (1989). *Evaluability assessment: A practical approach.* Boston: Kluwer.

Suarez-Balcazar, Y., & Orellana-Damacela, L. (1999). A university-community partnership for empowerment evaluation in a community housing organization. *Sociological Practice: A Journal of Clinical and Applied Sociology, 1*, 115-132.
Ury, W., Brett, J., & Goldberg, S. (1988). *Getting disputes resolved: Designing systems to cut the costs of conflict*. San Francisco: Jossey-Bass.
Webster, D. W. (1993, Winter). The unconvincing case for school-based conflict resolution programs for adolescents. *Health Affairs, 12*, 126-141.
Wholey, J. S. (1987). Evaluability assessment: Developing program theory. *New Directions for Program Evaluation, 33*, 45-62.

Empowerment Evaluation
of a Youth Leadership Training Program

Aparna Sharma

Loyola University Chicago

Yolanda Suarez-Balcazar

University of Illinois at Chicago

Matthew Baetke

The American Red Cross of Greater Chicago

SUMMARY. Due to budgetary constraints, many human service agencies are recruiting volunteers to supplement service delivery. A volunteer seeks out opportunities, in a planned manner, to help other individuals and/or groups of individuals. This paper illustrates an empowerment evaluation case study. Wandersman et al.'s (2004) empowerment evaluation principles are used to promote evaluation of the American Red Cross of

---

Address correspondence to: Aparna Sharma, Center for Urban Research and Learning, Loyola University Chicago, 820 North Michigan Avenue, Chicago, IL 60611-2196 (E-mail: *asharma@luc.edu*).

This project was funded in part by a grant from BP Social Global Investment to Loyola University Chicago.

[Haworth co-indexing entry note]: "Empowerment Evaluation of a Youth Leadership Training Program." Sharma, Aparna, Yolanda Suarez-Balcazar, and Matthew Baetke. Co-published simultaneously in *Journal of Prevention & Intervention in the Community* (The Haworth Press, Inc.) Vol. 26, No. 2, 2003, pp. 89-103; and: *Empowerment and Participatory Evaluation of Community Interventions: Multiple Benefits* (ed: Yolanda Suarez-Balcazar, and Gary W. Harper) The Haworth Press, Inc., 2003, pp. 89-103. Single or multiple copies of this article are available for a fee from The Haworth Document Delivery Service [1-800-HAWORTH, 9:00 a.m. - 5:00 p.m. (EST). E-mail address: docdelivery@haworthpress.com].

Greater Chicago's Youth Leadership Training Series, a program designed to train youth volunteers. *[Article copies available for a fee from The Haworth Document Delivery Service: 1-800-HAWORTH. E-mail address: <docdelivery@ haworthpress.com> Website: <http://www.HaworthPress.com> © 2003 by The Haworth Press, Inc. All rights reserved.]*

KEYWORDS. Youth leadership, empowerment evaluation, voluntarism

Many human service agencies are facing budgetary constraints for a variety of reasons, including a higher demand for services and a diminishing pool of available resources (e.g., money, space, and time). A trend within many of these agencies is to recruit volunteers to supplement service delivery. A volunteer seeks out opportunities to help individuals and/or groups in a planned manner (Clary & Snyder, 1991). Generally, the agencies and its volunteers set the length and the intensity of their involvement and determine how the volunteer's experiences can fit their own needs. Volunteerism involves a complex set of behaviors that fulfill several functions for individuals, including altruistic concerns, a sense of social responsibility, coping with internal conflicts, and gaining further knowledge and skills (Clary & Snyder, 1991; Omoto & Snyder, 1995; Schondel, Shields, & Orel, 1992).

The American Red Cross of Greater Chicago (ARCGC) Youth Leadership Training Series (YLTS) is a training program that teaches high school students how to become volunteer peer educators within specialized areas of prevention/health promotion. The YLTS program provides youth with the opportunity to increase their knowledge in a specialized interest area and develop the public speaking and facilitation skills necessary to teach fellow community members about topics such as HIV prevention, water safety, and disaster preparedness. The ARCGC collaborates with numerous high schools around the Chicago area to recruit students for this training. One of the long-term goals of this program is to motivate adolescents to become active volunteers in their community, which often leads to increased citizen participation (Omoto & Snyder, 1995). Little research has been conducted to examine the impact that programs such as the Red Cross YLTS have upon adolescents' motivation to volunteer and their level of volunteer-related skills. By examining a young adult's motivation to volunteer and any changes that occur as a result of volunteering (e.g., knowledge gained), we can better understand the impact of these programs upon youth and identify any relevant factors that can increase motivation to volunteer.

Researchers used an empowerment approach to assist the ARCGC staff in gaining evaluation skills and developing tools and procedures for improving their YLTS program (see Suarez-Balcazar, Orellana-Damacela, Portillo, Sharma, & Lanum, 2003). Empowerment evaluation is designed to increase the capacity of community stakeholders to make decisions about their program (Fawcett et al., 1996; Fetterman, Kaftarian, & Wandersman, 1996; Suarez-Balcazar & Orellana-Damacela, 1999; Wandersman, 1999; and Wandersman et al., 2004). Some of the goals of empowerment evaluation are to create a culture of learning within the organization and enhance the capacity of program stakeholders to take decisions that impact the program (Fetterman, 2002). The purpose of the evaluation project was to assist the YLTS staff in evaluating their program and transfer evaluation skills so that the staff could incorporate evaluation in their regular programming without the assistance of the researchers. A team was formed composed of two university researchers and three staff from ARCGC, one of whom became the primary contact. This person was familiar with evaluation methods and was interested in gaining more evaluation skills. In the following case study, we discuss the role of team members and the processes involved in the evaluation of the youth program.

CASE STUDY:
AN EMPOWERMENT EVALUATION
OF THE YOUTH LEADERSHIP TRAINING

Planning the Evaluation

The collaborative team adhered to the principles of university-community partnerships articulated by several researchers (see Cousins, Donahue, & Bloom, 1996; Harper & Salina, 2000; Kaftarian & Hansen, 1994; Roussos & Fawcett, 2000; Suarez-Balcazar et al., 2004) in which a trustful and respectful relationship was developed with the ARCGC staff.

The team met several times to review evaluation concepts, program goals and expectations. In addition, one of the key staff members attended an evaluation workshop organized by the researchers for a group of community-based organizations' staff. We will use Wandersman et al.'s (2004) 10 principles of empowerment evaluation to illustrate the building of evaluation capacity in the ARCGC staff. Table 1 lists the

TABLE 1

Empowerment Evaluation Principles	Specific Activities
1. Aims to influence the quality of programs	Instructor trainers' guide redesigned so that certain areas of the curriculum were highlighted for additional emphasis while others were earmarked for more cursory coverage.
2. The power and responsibility for evaluation lies with program stakeholders	Program staff decided on the key indicators to measure, shaped the development of the tools, decided which groups to collect data from and collected the data themselves.
3. Adheres to Evaluation Standards	In the planning stage of the evaluation, stakeholders and researcher discuss and plan for several standards including utility, feasibility, propriety, and accuracy standards.
4. Demystify evaluation	At the beginning of the project, two stakeholders attended an empowerment evaluation workshop in which myths and fears were discussed.
5. Emphasize collaboration with program stakeholders	The university researchers and ARCGC staff worked together in every phase of the process. Staff took the lead in refining the original evaluation measure at the end of this evaluation project.
6. Builds stakeholders' capacity to conduct evaluation and to effectively use results	To build capacity for evaluation, the research team conducted several group (e.g., evaluation workshop, brainstorming outcomes training) and one-on-one activities (training on data entry using SPSS, and data analysis).
7. Use evaluation results to improve program	ARCGC's built case statements for program funding. To date, the ARCGC has shared this information with corporations, foundations and several major donors to solicit ongoing financial support for its YLTS program.
8. Can be implemented at any stage of program development.	Stakeholders implement the Youth Leadership program continuously in high schools. The evaluation started at the beginning of a new cohort of schools and is going on continuously.
9. Influences program planning	ARCGC was able to use the research to effectively streamline and improve its instructor training (peer educator training) processes.
10. Institutionalizes self-evaluation among program staff	After minor changes were done to the evaluation tools, the CBO is engaging in ongoing evaluation of their program.

Taken from Wandersman et al. (2004). In L. Jason, K. Keys, Y. Suarez-Balcazar, M. Davis, J. Durlak, & D. Isenberg. *Participatory Community Research: Theories and Methods in Action.* Copyright © 2004 by the American Psychological Association. Adapted with permission.

principles and the activities and processes involved in the empower-ment evaluation of YLTS. According to Wandersman et al. (2004), empowerment evaluation aims to influence the quality of the program, give power over the evaluation to the stakeholders, follow evaluation standards, demystify evaluation, emphasize collaboration, build stakeholders capacity, and facilitate the use of evaluation results to improve the program. Empowerment evaluation processes can be implemented at any stage of the program, and hold the potential to influence program planning and institutionalize evaluation standards among the stakeholders (Wandersman et al.).

The planning stage was also an opportunity to discuss fears and myths about evaluation. The ARCGC staff had both positive and negative experiences working with other evaluators, who conducted evaluations of similar programs. Staff members had an opportunity to discuss these issues openly with the researchers. Researchers facilitated several brainstorming sessions about the YLTS program goals, activities, objectives, outcomes, and impact. These discussion sessions allowed the team to reflect on the program and select key indicators. The evaluation team agreed that the YLTS program was designed to impact youth motivation to volunteer, knowledge about specific topics, and increase positive volunteering experiences (see Clary & Snyder, 1991; Cnann & Goldberg-Glenn, 1991; Omoto & Snyder, 1995 for a review of motivation to volunteer).

ROLES AND PROCESSES INVOLVED
IN THE METHODOLOGY

Selection of Participants

Consistent with the previously mentioned empowerment evaluation principles, the ARCGC staff had the responsibility of selecting the participants and settings for this pilot evaluation project. The selection of participants was discussed with the researchers who provided feedback but ultimately selection was under the control of the ARCGC staff.

This evaluation was implemented with a group of YLTS participants from two different high schools. This group consisted of high-school students who participated in either the Whales Tales (WT, a water safety education for children) or Community Disaster Education (CDE). Participants signed up for the YLTS training at their local high schools. Participants were predominantly Caucasian (64% Caucasian, 13% African American, 10% Hispanic and 13% other) and mostly female (68% female, 32% male). In the selection of participants for the pilot evaluation, ARCGC staff considered a few variables including timing (schools they had promised training and were ready for the Red Cross staff to begin), willingness of the schools to participate, and geographical location of schools.

Procedure

The ARCGC staff and the researchers played different roles during the selection of the YLTS evaluation procedures. For example, the ARCGC worked with the high school staff to determine the appropriate times to administer the evaluation surveys. The team discussed different ways in which the assessments could be conducted and negotiated the appropriate possible procedure with the school. It is important to mention that the ARCGC staff did not have absolute control during this phase and depended on the schools availability. During this phase, the role of the university research partners primarily consisted of consulting and advising, listening to different points of view about procedural issues, and facilitating the process. The Red Cross staff administered the surveys before and after the training. Training consisted of an eight-hour session taught by the ARCGC staff either in one full school day or over several school days (the schedule was determined by the participating high school). During training, 94 participants learned about the Red Cross, about voluntarism, how to be a volunteer in their communities, and specific knowledge about water safety, and how to respond to disasters such as inundations.

Design

A time series design was used to evaluate the YLTS program based on decisions taken by the team after many discussions. The Whales Tales group (WT), which began in Spring 2001, was assessed at several different time periods: Pre-training, post-training, 1 month post-training, and 6 months post-training. The Community Disaster Education group (CDE), which began in Fall 2001, was assessed only at pre- and post-training. Not all of the WT and CDE participants completed evaluation assessments at one-month and six-month follow-up. A total of 44 participants from the WT program completed a pre-training assessment, which was administered immediately before the training program began, and a post-training assessment, which was administered immediately after the one-day training program ended. There were nine WT participants who completed a one-month follow-up survey and eleven participants who completed the six-month follow-up survey. A total of 50 participants from the Community Disaster Education (CDE) program completed the pre-training and post-training assessments.

The number of participants captured for each of the assessments was not under the control of the researchers or ARCGC staff but depended on the individual choice of the participants. However, the ARCGC staff played a key role planning for the assessments, contacting the schools, obtaining permissions from the schools, and collecting data. The researchers advised as necessary and were minimally involved in this phase.

Evaluation Measures

The ARCGC staff played a very critical role during the selection of indicators and assessment measures. Consistent with empowerment evaluation principles, the evaluation team built capacity within the organization by facilitating the process of selecting indicators and developing a program logic model (see logic model in Milstein & Chapel, 2002; Weiss, 1995). For instance, all of the evaluation measures were identified and developed using a multi-method approach including a review of the literature, by extensive brainstorming sessions with the ARCGC Youth Education staff, and through working sessions in which the measuring tools were refined and adapted to the needs of the program. The third author was the primary contact and ensured that the rest of the ARCGC staff were regularly updated with revised drafts of the evaluation measures with the hope of keeping the ARCGC staff invested in this phase of the evaluation. For example, several of the ARCGC staff developed the knowledge questions for the curriculum-based measure in collaboration with the first author. The selection of measurement tools is often one of the challenges of empowerment evaluation. Here, the partnership team had to constantly balance evaluation standards and scientific merit versus needs and resources of the agency. Consistent with the empowerment evaluation principle of assuring adoption of evaluation methods (Wandersman et al., 2004), the staff were very careful about selecting measures that assessed the objectives of the program, as well as measures that they understood well, liked, and thought were appropriate and were willing to use them again. Based on an ongoing collaboration process, the following measures were selected and developed by the team.

Motivation to volunteer. Prior to beginning the YLTS program, all students were given a pre-training survey that asked participants to rate their motivations to volunteer. The motivation to volunteer scale created by Omoto and Snyder (1995) had five sub-scales (values, personal development, understanding, community concern, and esteem enhancement) that were found to have relatively high Cronbach alpha's (.74, .80, .77, .82, and .80, respectively). The ARCGC examined the Omoto and Snyder measure and adapted 24 of the original scale's items in order to reflect how the proposed functions of volunteerism related to the YLTS program. Participants were asked to rate their opinion on statements pertaining to volunteerism. They rated the statements using a 4-point Likert-type scale (1 = Strongly Disagree; 2 = Disagree; 3 = Agree; 4 = Strongly Agree). Examples of questions included: "Volunteering will make me feel good about myself" and "I can make a difference in my community."

Knowledge assessment. All YLTS participants were also asked to answer questions pertaining to their specialty track in order to test their knowledge before and after training and during the six-month follow-up. This assessment was given in the form of multiple-choice questions, which were designed to measure the degree to which youth participants grasped the curriculum concepts covered by the trainer. Such an assessment of knowledge is mandatory for all "Red Cross Health and Safety" education courses. The highest possible score for the knowledge measure is 15, which indicates that the participant answered all of the multiple-choice questions correctly. All of these questions were based on the curriculum taught in this leadership course. The Red Cross staff helped develop a database of questions that reflected all specialty areas taught including: (a) curriculum specific knowledge such as a case of "fire" emergency scenario; (b) questions relating to effective teaching methods needed for presentations, also called the Instructor Candidate Training such as how to present information to kids about water safety; and (c) questions relating to general Red Cross history such as goals, mission, and programs of the Red Cross. Each of these three sections had five questions for a total of 15 knowledge questions.

Satisfaction survey. A 15-item satisfaction survey, developed by the evaluation team, was administered to all YLTS participants once the in-class training session was completed. Participants were asked to rate their satisfaction with different aspects of the training using a 4-point Likert-type scale (1 = Strongly Disagree; 2 = Disagree; 3 = Agree; 4 = Strongly Agree).

Number of volunteer activities. While the ARCGC staff coordinated and collected the data at one-month follow-up, the first author coordinated and collected the 6-month follow-up data via telephone interviews of former YLTS participants. At the 6-month follow-up assessment, in addition to administering the knowledge, motivation, and satisfaction scales, the WT participants were asked to list the volunteer activities they participated in over the last 6 months since training completion.

CASE STUDY RESULTS

The planning for the data analysis took place between the evaluators and the ARCGC staff while we entered completed surveys using SPSS software. The authors decided on what relationships to examine between the measured variables and proceeded to conduct the preliminary data analysis together. Once the data was analyzed, the team presented and discussed the findings with all ARCGC staff on an on-going basis for comments.

Pre-Post Differences in Motivation to Volunteer and Knowledge Scores

The analyses focused on the within-subjects differences for the key variables: knowledge and motivation to volunteer. As seen in Table 2, there was a significant difference in overall knowledge gain with the exception of the Instructor Candidate Training (ICT) knowledge sub-scale items. In the post-assessment, this gain in knowledge was expected and indicates that the participants retained some of the information provided in the training program. The Instructor Candidate portion of the YLTS program was the only part of the training curriculum on which the participants did not significantly improve after training. The overall gain in knowledge increased from 6.88 correct answers to 9.49 correct answers out of 15 questions. Although this is a statistically significant difference, the post-training knowledge scores are relatively low (raw

TABLE 2. Mean Pre-Post Differences (N = 94)

Pre-Post Variables	Mean	SD	t	df	p
Knowledge					
Total Score	2.61	2.88	8.52	87	.001
Curriculum	2.00	1.91	9.84	87	.001
Red Cross History	0.61	1.36	4.23	87	.001
Instructor Training	0.06	1.54	0.38	87	.73
Motivation to Volunteer					
Total Score	1.35	4.36	2.67	73	.01
Self-Enhancement	0.90	2.17	3.71	79	.001
Altruistic	0.22	1.68	1.23	84	.22
Social	0.79	1.80	3.95	80	.001

score = 63.27%; corrected for guessing = 50.8%). This could be due to the knowledge measure's inability to test the material being taught in the program or it could be that the program was not effectively relaying the YLTS curriculum to its participants.

Participants exhibited a significant increase in overall motivation to volunteer after participating in the YLTS training. Upon closer examination of the motivation sub-scales, it is evident that participants did not significantly increase their "altruistic" motivation to volunteer.

Follow-Up on the Whales Tales Group

One of the challenges that the evaluation team faced was the lack of staff from the Red Cross to carry on multiple training sessions or to visit other high schools to conduct assessments from participants (e.g., comparison group). Consequently, the team decided to add a one- and six-month follow-up assessment to the Whales Tales group evaluation. Of the participants who completed a pre- and post-training assessment, 10 completed a one-month follow-up assessment and 11 completed a six-month follow-up assessment.

A series of paired sample t-tests were conducted between pre-training and one-month and six-month follow-up and between post-training and six-month follow-up. As indicated in Table 3, there was no significant change in the participants' motivation to volunteer from pre-training to one month and pre-training to six months (n = 9) after the completion of

TABLE 3. Mean Differences for All Pre-Training–Follow-up Variables*

Pre-Post Variables	Mean	SD	t	df	p
Motivation to Volunteer					
Pre training-1 month	3.10	4.89	−2.01	9	0.08
Pre training-6 months	0.28	6.59	0.14	10	0.90
Knowledge					
Post training-6 months	7.67	1.94	11.88	8	0.01
Number of Volunteer Activities					
Pre training-6 months	1.2	1.69	2.25	9	0.05

* Only WT Participants

the training program. However, the six-month follow-up assessments of knowledge and number of volunteer activities yielded significant differences (n = 11). Not all participants in the training completed a follow-up assessment for many reasons, including not being available on the day of the assessment or no longer attending the high school. In addition, students who completed the follow-up assessment had engaged in a significant number of volunteer activities. This in itself was a very important result for the Red Cross staff as they emphasize the importance of volunteering during training. Overall, participants were very satisfied with the training they received.

Building Capacity and Institutionalizing Evaluation

One of the products of this evaluation was the development of an assessment instrument that the Red Cross staff would use consistently to evaluate the YLTS program. At the end of this pilot case study, the evaluation team refined the original evaluation measures. We examined the correlation matrices for each of the measures and items with very high inter-correlations (i.e., above .70) were omitted as well as items with very low correlations. The evaluation team also decided to shorten the knowledge assessment (from 15 to 6 items). The ARCGC staff was very knowledgeable with regard to evaluating program impact and this partnership was able to enhance the staff's evaluation protocols with additional resources. For example, the team also held several working sessions on how to develop a database for evaluation results as well as how to analyze and interpret new data using the pilot evaluation data as a template.

Uses of the Evaluation Results

As with any evaluation, it is important to design tools that yield information that can be utilized on an instrumental and conceptual level. The Red Cross staff was able to apply the evaluation findings from this study to demonstrate both levels of research utilization, instrumental and conceptual utilization (Leviton & Hughes, 1981). In terms of instrumental utilization, the ARCGC staff used the research to effectively streamline and improve its instructor training (peer educator training) processes. The evaluation process led to the redesigning of the instructor trainer's guide, whereby certain areas of the curriculum were highlighted for additional emphasis while others were earmarked for more cursory coverage. This enabled program staff to better allocate training time to maximize their impact on program participants. On a conceptual level, the program staff utilized the information to validate the successful implementation of the program and to document its impact. As part of the ARCGC's work performance management processes, program managers are evaluated on the degree to which they successfully implement their program. At the time, the ARCGC's manager of planning and evaluation is exploring methods of linking outcome based evaluation implementation to an individual's work performance. Another example of conceptual utilization is ARCGC's ability to utilize these results to build "success story" statements for program funding. To date, the American Red Cross of Greater Chicago has shared information about its programs with corporations, foundations and several major donors to solicit ongoing financial support for its YLTS program.

DISCUSSION

One of the main goals of this project was to assist the staff in developing tools and protocols that they could use on a regular basis and conduct a pilot evaluation of their YLTS program. Guided by these goals, there were multiple benefits that resulted from this collaboration. First, the ARCGC staff now utilizes a set of measures in which they played a critical role in selecting, adapting, developing and pilot-testing tools. Second, this pilot study allowed the ARC staff to learn about the impact of their YLTS program, and they have implemented changes according to the results and observations gathered. Third, the ARCGC staff has presented these evaluation findings and protocols to potential funders to garner additional financial support for the YLTS program.

This case study illustrates empowerment evaluation in action and provided the staff with some useful results. One of the goals of the YLTS program is to have the participants continue to teach fellow community members what they have learned in the training program, establishing opportunities for the youth to present at other venues and encouraging volunteerism in youth. The youth in the WT group did not make any more community presentations after the initial presentation on National Youth Service Day. This might explain the return to pre-training motivation scores. Despite this, we found that participants engaged in more volunteer activities. While there was no increase in the participants' motivation-to-volunteer score at follow-up, they were involved in significantly more volunteer activities after participating in the YLTS program than prior to participating in the program. This finding suggests that participants maintained an interest in volunteering after completing the program. This is a positive finding and the Red Cross staff should take advantage of this increased interest in volunteerism and initiate follow-up contact with participants in order to maintain an active roster of youth volunteers. Follow-up phone calls had not been conducted before this project and provided the staff an easy method of assessing the impact of the training and encouraging volunteer activities in youth's communities, which is one of the main goals of the youth leadership training. Red Cross staff is currently discussing what realistic expectations from participants are and what role the staff might play in encouraging voluntarism and community presentations among participants.

Overall, according to the staff, one of the aspects they benefited the most out of the evaluation project was not only the increased capacity and self-determination but also the identification of key indicators and development of tools. The staff invested a lot of effort in refining the measurement tools; since the completion of this evaluation, the original evaluation measures have been refined according to emerging needs of the YLTS program staff. The new evaluation measure includes shortened knowledge, satisfaction, and motivation-to-volunteer scales. This also led to some reflection; given the low means for the post-training knowledge score, the staff is examining closely how the YLTS curriculum was being taught to the participants and whether any programmatic changes are required. The ARCGC staff have committed to using the refined evaluation measure in full for every third YLTS group they organize (the Red Cross averages one YLTS class/month) and has committed to using the satisfaction survey for every YLTS group they organize. The goal of the ARCGC evaluation team is to institutionalize evaluation of the YLTS in the hopes of garnering future funding to expand the program.

This evaluation of the YLTS program employed original measures in addition to scales adapted for this purpose. The knowledge scale, for instance, was developed by the team and designed to fit the YLTS program goals. As with any new measure, future research needs to address the reliability and validity of the scales. This will likely shed more light on the usefulness of these evaluation measures. However, as we learned through this project, the tools need to have face and social validity. That is, they need to "mean something" to the staff and participants. Measurement tools are useful as long as the staff can use them, as long as the tools measure what they are intended to measure, and as long as they advance the goals of empowerment evaluation; which is to foster program improvement and self-determination.

Despite the benefits to the organization there were some limitations in this case study. The evaluation team was unable to employ a control or comparison group, a limitation that is typical of participatory community research of this nature (Dalton, Elias & Wandersman, 2001). The use of a comparison group could have addressed internal validity threats such as history. The results of this initial study should be used as a comparison against future YLTS groups following the implementation of the program changes that were suggested by the evaluation. This issue was discussed with the staff and they believe that despite the limitations of the study, they were able to gain knowledge and insight about their program and appreciated the opportunity to reflect about the program in order to make improvements. This actually motivated them to continue improving their evaluations. The staff saw this as an occasion to adopt evaluation procedures as part of their daily activities.

We believe that although we are still learning about how to implement empowerment evaluation, we created a culture of learning about evaluation knowledge and skills at the American Red Cross. The researchers maintain contact with the staff a year after this project was completed, and the staff is still using the guide and learning about how to improve their program. In fact, evaluation became part of their regular programming.

REFERENCES

Clary, E. G., & Snyder, M. (1991). A functional analysis of altruism and prosocial behavior: The case of volunteerism. In M.S. Clark (Ed.), *Review of Personality and Social Psychology* (Vol. 12, pp. 119-148). Newbury Park, CA: Sage.

Cnnan, R. A., & Goldberg-Glen, R. S. (1991). Measuring motivation to volunteer in human services. *Journal of Applied Behavioral Science, 27,* 269-284.

Cousins, J. B., Donohue, J. J., & Bloom, G. A. (1996). Collaborative evaluation in North America: Evaluators' self-reported opinions, practices and consequences. *Evaluation Practice, 17,* 207-226.

Dalton, J. H., Elias, M. J., & Wandersman, A. (2001). *Community psychology: Linking individuals and communities.* Belmont, CA: Wadsworth.

Fawcett, S. B., Paine-Andrews, A., Francisco, V. T., Schultz, J. A., Richter, K. P., Lewis, R. K. et al. (1996). Empowering community health initiatives through evaluation. In D. Fetterman, S. Kaftarian, & A. Wandersman (Eds.), *Empowerment evaluation: Knowledge and tools for self-assessment and accountability* (pp. 256- 276). Thousand Oaks, CA: Sage.

Fetterman, D., M. (2002). Empowerment Evaluation: Building communities of practice and a culture of learning. *American Journal of Community Psychology, 30,* 89-102.

Fetterman, D. Kaftarian, S. & Wandersman, A. (Eds.) (1996). *Empowerment evaluation: Knowledge and tools for self-assessment and accountability*. Thousand Oaks, CA: Sage.

Harper, G. W., & Salina, D. D. (2000). Building collaborative partnerships to improve community-based HIV prevention research: The university-CBO collaborative partnership (UCCP) model. *Journal of Prevention & Intervention in the Community, 19*, 1-20.

Kaftarian, J., & Hansen, W. B. (Eds.). (1994). Community Partnership Program (CSAP special issue). *Journal of Community Psychology, 22*.

Leviton, L., & Hughes, E. (1981). Research on the utilization of evaluation. A review and synthesis. *Evaluation Review, 5*, 525-548.

Milstein, B., & Chapel, T. (2002). Developing a logic model or theory of change. *Community Tool Box*, chapter 2: section 7. Retrieved from *http://ctb.ku.edu/tools/EN/chapter_1002.htm*.

Omoto, A. M., & Snyder, M. (1995). Sustained helping without obligation: Motivation, longevity of service, and perceived attitude change among AIDS volunteers. *Journal of Personality and Social Psychology, 68*, 671-686.

Roussos, S. T., & Fawcett, S. B. (2000). A review of collaborative partnerships as a strategy for improving community health. *Annual Review of Public Health, 21*, 369-402.

Schondel, C., Shields, G., & Orel, N. (1992). Development of an instrument to measure volunteers' motivation in working with people with AIDS. *Social Work in Health Care, 17*, 53-71.

Suarez-Balcazar, Y., & Orellana-Damacela, L. (1999). A university-community partnership for empowerment evaluation in a community housing organization. *Sociological Practice: A Journal of Clinical and Applied Research, 1*, 115-132.

Suarez-Balcazar, Y., Davis, M., Ferrari, J., Nyden, P., Olson, B., Alvarez, J., Molloy, P., & Toro, P. (2004). University-community partnerships: A framework and an exemplar. In L. Jason, K. Keys, Y. Suarez-Balcazar, M. Davis, J. Durlak, & D. Isenberg. *Participatory community research: Theories and methods in action*. Washington, DC: American Psychological Association.

Suarez-Balcazar, Y., Orellana-Damacela, L., Portillo, N., Sharma, A., & Lanum, M. (2003). Implementing and outcomes framework in the empowerment and participatory evaluation of community initiatives. *Journal of Prevention & Intervention in the Community, 26*, 5-20.

Wandersman, A. (1999). Framing the evaluation of health and human service programs in community settings: Assessing progress. In J. Telfair & L. C. Merchant (Eds.), *New Directions for Evaluation: Evaluating health and human service programs in community settings* (Vol. 83). American Evaluation Association: Jossey-Bass.

Wandersman, A., Keener, D., Snell-Johns, J., Miller, R., Flaspohler, P., Livet-Dye, M., Mendez, J., Behrens, T., Bolson, B., & Robinson, L. (2004). In L. Jason, K. Keys, Y. Suarez-Balcazar, M. Davis, J. Durlak, & D. Isenberg. *Participatory community research: Theories and methods in action*. Washington, DC: American Psychological Association.

Weiss, C. H. (1995). Nothing as practical as good theory: Exploring theory-based evaluation for comprehensive community initiatives for children and families. In J. P. Connell, A. Kubisch, L. Schorr, & C. H. Weiss (Eds.), *New approaches to evaluating community initiatives: Concepts, methods, and contexts* (pp. 65-92). Washington, DC: The Aspen Institute.

Strategies for Needs Assessment in Prevention, edited by Alex Zautra, Kenneth Bachrach, and Robert E. Hess, PhD* (Vol. 2, No. 4, 1983). *"An excellent survey on applied techniques for doing needs assessments. . . . It should be on the shelf of anyone involved in prevention." (Journal of Pediatric Psychology)*

Innovations in Prevention, edited by Robert E. Hess, PhD, and Jared Hermalin, PhD* (Vol. 2, No. 3, 1983). *An exciting book that provides invaluable insights on effective prevention programs.*

Rx Television: Enhancing the Preventive Impact of TV, edited by Joyce Sprafkin, Carolyn Swift, PhD, and Robert E. Hess, PhD* (Vol. 2, No. 1/2, 1983). *"The successful interventions reported in this volume make interesting reading on two grounds. First, they show quite clearly how powerful television can be in molding children. Second, they illustrate how this power can be used for good ends." (Contemporary Psychology)*

Early Intervention Programs for Infants, edited by Howard A. Moss, MD, Robert E. Hess, PhD, and Carolyn Swift, PhD* (Vol. 1, No. 4, 1982). *"A useful resource book for those child psychiatrists, paediatricians, and psychologists interested in early intervention and prevention." (The Royal College of Psychiatrists)*

Helping People to Help Themselves: Self-Help and Prevention, edited by Leonard D. Borman, PhD, Leslie E. Borck, PhD, Robert E. Hess, PhD, and Frank L. Pasquale* (Vol. 1, No. 3, 1982). *"A timely volume . . . a mine of information for interested clinicians, and should stimulate those wishing to do systematic research in the self-help area." (The Journal of Nervous and Mental Disease)*

Evaluation and Prevention in Human Services, edited by Jared Hermalin, PhD, and Jonathan A. Morell, PhD* (Vol. 1, No. 1/2, 1982). *Features methods and problems related to the evaluation of prevention programs.*

Index

Accountability systems
    First Steps, 42-49
        coordination, 47
        organizational structure, 47
        progress and lessons, 46
Action planning, community change, 30
Acquired immunodeficiency syndrome
        (AIDS)
    risk reduction model, 63
    see also HIV prevention
Adolescent pregnancy, community
        initiatives, 30
African-Americans, HIV prevention, 65
American Red Cross
    empowerment evaluation, 89
    youth leadership training, 90
Aspen Roundtable (2002), 40
Audiotapes, collaborative process, 61

Behavioral surveys, 28
Brainstorming, outcomes model, 10

California, early childhood initiatives, 39
Capacity building
    case examples, 25
    community initiatives, 21-34
    data interpretation, 30
    Kansas models, 25
    logic model, 26
    participatory evaluation, 21-34
    televised events, 25
    Web site, 25
Centers for Disease Control and
        Prevention, 28
Chicago
    American Red Cross, 90
    empowerment evaluation, 90

HIV prevention, 56
    youth leadership training, 90
Chronic Disease Coalition, outcomes
        model, 26
Collaborative process
    benefits, 66
    community relevance, 53
    cultural appropriateness, 53
    evaluation, 53,55
    HIV prevention, 53
    Implementation, 60-62
    outreach monitoring, 59
    partnership development, 57
    plan and methods, 58-62
    program changes, 62-66
    promotion, 59
    skill inhancement, 58
    theoretical foundations, 56
Collaborative programs
    case study, 71-85
    changes, 62-66
    conflict resolution, 71
    development phases, 75-82
    lessons learned, 83-85
    project overview, 74
Committee on Integrating the Science
        of Early Childhood
        Development (2000), 39
Community-based organizations (CBO)
    additional funding, 18
    challenges and solutions, 9
    collaborative process, 53,55
    cultural appropriateness, 53
    data collection, 11-13
    development, 10
    empowerment, 1-3
    enhancing relevance, 53
    evaluation phases, 8-10
    HIV prevention, 53

implementation, 5-18
interpreting findings, 13
methodology, 11-13
outcomes model, 5-18
participatory evaluation, 1,5
staff turnover, 9
tools and protocols, 12
United Way model, 5,7
utilization findings, 15
Community initiatives
accountability, 37-50
capacity building, 21-34
celebrating success, 31
defined, 50
empowerment evaluation, 41
evaluation challenges, 40
framework and supports, 24-32
intervention, 28
large-scale, 39
making adjustments, 31
participatory evaluation, 21-34
progress and lessons, 46
promoting programs, 37
statewide, 37-50
Community Tool Box (Web site), 25,30
Comprehensive community initiatives,
50
Conflict resolution education (CRE)
collaborative program, 71
commercial programs, 83
logic model, 76
meta-analysis, 81
preliminary results, 81
self-control, 76
Conflict Resolution in Schools
Program (CRiSP)
case study, 73
collaborative program, 71
community initiative, 71
component sufficiency, 78
conditional effects, 82
design and implementation, 77
development phases, 75-82
elementary schools, 77
evaluability issues, 75,78
high schools, 78

identifying needs, 75-77
lessons learned, 83-85
logic model, 75
meta-analysis, 80
middle schools, 77
performance criteria, 79
problem-solving, 76
project overview, 74
research methods, 74,80
resource adequacy, 79
situation analyses, 76
stakeholder groups, 74
target schools, 77
Consortium on Negotiation and
Conflict Resolution, 73,84
Cultural appropriateness, HIV
prevention, 53

Data collection, outcomes model, 11-13
DePaul University, HIV prevention, 56

Early childhood, community
initiatives, 37-50
Early intervention, 80,85
Effective practice experts (EPE), 44
Elementary schools, CRiSP
implementation, 77
Empowerment
community organizations, 1-3
female, 64
participatory evaluation, 1-3
programs, 37-50
theory, 2
Empowerment evaluation
case study, 91-93
collaborative programs, 75
community initiatives, 41
defined, 41
mystification problem, 9
outcomes model, 7
planning, 91-93
principles and activities, 92
programs, 37-50
results and uses, 14,99

youth leadership training, 89-102
Empowerment Evaluation (Fetterman), 2
Empowerment Theory (Zimmerman), 2

First Steps, accountability system, 42-49
Florida, early childhood initiatives, 39
Focus groups, collaborative process, 60

Gay-bisexual-questioning (GBQ)
    HIV prevention, 56
    program changes, 63,65
Goal framing, problem naming, 25
Government Performance and Results
        Act (1993), 40

High schools, CRiSP implementation, 78
HIV prevention
    collaborative process, 53-68
    community relevance, 53
    dating and relationships, 64
    group intervention, 65
    program changes, 62-66
    sexual health programs, 63

Instructor candidate training (ICT), 97
Instrumental utilization, outcomes
        model, 29
Interventions, documenting, 28

Kansas, capacity building models, 25

Latino youth, HIV prevention, 56,65
Leadership. *See* Youth leadership
        training
Logic model, participatory evaluation, 22

Meta-analysis, CRiSP model, 80
Middle schools

CRiSP implementation, 77
    evaluability issues, 78
Multiple stakeholders, program
        evaluation, 48

National Association for Mediation
        in Education, 74
National Education Goals Panel
        (1991), 40
National Governors Association
        (2000), 40
National Turning Point, community
        initiative, 29
National Youth Service Day, 100
No Child Left Behind Act (2002), 39
Nonparticipant observations,
        collaborative process, 61
North Carolina
    early childhood initiatives, 39
    Smart Start program, 42

Outcomes model
    challenges and solutions, 9
    community organizations, 5-18
    conceptual utilization, 15
    data collection, 11-13
    development, 10
    evaluation process, 8,14
    implementation, 5-18
    interpreting findings, 13
    measurement system, 6
    methodology, 11-13
    participatory evaluation, 5-18
    tools and protocols, 12
Outreach monitoring, collaborative
        process, 59
Outside experts, participatory
        evaluation, 23
Participatory Action Research
        (Jason), 2
Participatory evaluation
    capacity building, 21-34
    challenges and benefits, 32

community organizations, 1,5,21
  development, 8-10
  evaluation, 8-10
  framework and supports, 24-32
  logic model, 22
  outside experts, 23
  process-related issues, 16
Partnerships
  collaborative process, 57
  participatory evaluation, 6
  university, 18
Personal development, volunteer
    motivation, 95
Planning-implementation-evaluation
    (PIE)
  Accountability system, 43-48
  county example, 45
  evaluation coaching, 44
  shell and prototype, 43
Pregnancy. *See* Adolescent pregnancy
Problem naming, goal framing, 25
Psychology, community, 1
Public health, community initiative, 29

Qualitative interviews, collaborative
    process, 60

Research questions, outcomes model,
    27
Robert Wood Johnson Foundation, 29

Schools
  community initiatives, 37
  evaluating needs, 76
  readiness, 37
  see also Conflict Resolution in
    Schools Program
Session evaluation forms, 60
Skill enhancement, staff members, 58
Smart Start, North Carolina, 42
Social and rehabilitative services,
    outcomes model, 25

Social cognitive theory, HIV
    prevention, 63
Sociology, participatory action
    research, 2
South Carolina, First Steps program,
    42
Staff members
  collaborative process, 58
  skill enhancement, 58
  turnover challenge, 9
Stakeholders, multiple, 48
Statewide programs, community
    initiatives, 37
Structure analyses, collaborative
    process, 61
Symbolic utilization, outcomes model,
    15

Technical advisers, program
    evaluation, 44

United Way model, community
    organization, 5, 7
University-community partnership, 91

Value scale, volunteer motivation, 95
Volunteers
  community concern, 95
  esteem enhancement, 95
  number of activities, 96
  see also Youth leadership training

Web site, capacity building, 25
Whales Tales, water safety program,
    93,98
Women, empowerment, 64
Young Men's Program (YMP)
  HIV prevention, 56
  program changes, 62,65
Youth leadership training (YLT)
  capacity building, 99

case study, 91-93
empowerment evaluation, 89-102
evaluation measures, 95
institutionalizing evaluation, 99
knowledge assessment, 96
methodology, 93-96
motivating volunteers, 95,97
number of activities, 96
participant selection, 93
procedure and design, 94
program, 89-102
results, 97-100
roles and processes, 93-96
satisfaction survey, 96